WWW.PASSAICPUBLICLIBRARY.ORG
3 2344 09249427 1

D1407880

Jewish Traces in Unexpected Places

(and Unexpected Traces In Jewish Places)

Al Kustanowitz

COVER PHOTOS

Introduction and Acknowledgements

This book is based on some of the best of the hundreds of anecdotes that make up my blog, Jewish Humor Central (www.jewishhumorcentral.com).

Seven years ago I didn't know what a blog was. My daughter Esther, who has since built a career on blogging and social media, was very patient in explaining to me more than once exactly what she was doing writing one blog, then another, and another. Finally, I got it.

In October 2009, I had an idea. I have always felt that many of my Jewish friends, relatives, and especially professional Jews -- rabbis, cantors, etc. -- take themselves and their observance too seriously. Maybe the seriousness that pervades Jewish religious life in its many forms should be and could be tempered with a touch of humor here and there.

Wouldn't we all be happier and healthier (after all, laughter is the best medicine) if we started each day with a smile, laugh, or even just a grin of recognition at the funny happenings that we, our brethren, and *sistren* experience because of our Jewishness?

That's how the blog called Jewish Humor Central got started. Esther continues to be a strong supporter, and sometimes a source of new material. I also get great satisfaction and support from my sons Jack and Simmy and daughters-in-law Penina and Ilana, who were among the first of my thousands of subscribers around the world.

Finally, Jewish Humor Central would not exist without the loving support of my late wife Shulamit, who edited many of my blog entries and served as a gentle censor of some of the entries that might have otherwise entered the blogosphere with questionable content. This book is dedicated to her memory.

Table of Contents

Welcome to the World of Jewish Humor Central

I have been searching for Jewish humor on the Internet ever since the Internet began. You would think that with so many Jewish comedians doing stand-up, TV, and films, there would be an infinite number of web sites with high quality Jewish humor. Well, there aren't. Sure, you'll find some sites with old Jewish jokes, books of Jewish humor included in Amazon's collection, and some hilarious YouTube videos, but you're unlikely to find a single web site that reports regularly on lots of funny things that are happening now in the Jewish world, and also comments on a wide variety of things Jewish that bring a grin, smile, chuckle, laugh, guffaw, or sometimes a sigh to readers.

That's the mission that I undertook for the blog that I named Jewish Humor Central (www.jewishhumorcentral.com). Since starting the blog in October 2009, I have been focusing on Jewish humor in many categories including jokes, stories, parodies, satire, legends, books, films, unbelievable but true happenings, and funny incidents in the news. Some are new, and some are classics. A few are not really funny, but thought provoking. The blog posts include my own comments, but generally rely on the links to tell their own story.

The blog includes items from religious and secular sources of all Jewish denominations, and I strive to keep the site family-friendly. I do not set out to mock or slight any group or subgroup but I can’t guarantee that people without a sense of humor will not be offended by some of the posts or links.

So you might ask, “Why a book?” and “Why now?

The nature of a blog is that the many posts (now exceeding 1800) appear and disappear. Of course, if you want to take the time to search the archives and keywords on the Jewish Humor Central site, you can find any post going back to the first one. But very few people find the time to do this.

The overnight growth of tablets and smartphones presented an opportunity to organize the best posts by category, present them for display in color and in black-and-white with direct links to the videos and make them available to a wide audience at a very low price.

The first edition of this book was Volume 4 of a series titled Jewish Humor on Your Desktop, subtitled Jewish Traces in Unexpected Places. Unlike the other volumes, it isn't laughing out loud funny, although there are funny moments in some of the anecdotes and videos.

The book you're reading now is a major update and expansion of the original volume. Many new anecdotes and videos have been added, and it has been organized into sections based on geography.

The premise of the book is that we are familiar with Jewish life in all of the major cities around the world where Jews have settled and established a rich culture. But a Jewish presence shines through in some more remote areas of the globe and in cities where because of climate or politics it wouldn't be expected to thrive.

In researching material for this book, we discovered another group of anecdotes and videos that represent the other side of the unexpected – instances in which Jewish culture and other popular cultures come together in surprising ways. We treat these separately in Part two of the book, called Unexpected Traces in Jewish Places.

This book also includes links to more than 80 versions of the most popular Hebrew and Jewish songs as sung around the world -- Hava Nagila, Hevenu Shalom Aleichem, Hinei Ma Tov, Abanibi, and Tumbalalaika.

This book, all seven volumes of the original series, and the complete collection are available at Amazon.com. Here are the titles of the books in the original series:

Jewish Humor on Your Desktop
Vol. 1 - Old Jokes and New Comedians
Vol. 2 - Israel is a Funny Country (also available as an updated expanded edition)
Vol. 3 – Humor in Jewish Life: You Can't Make This Stuff Up
Vol. 4 – Jewish Traces in Unexpected Places
Vol. 5 – Yiddish is a Funny Language
Vol. 6 – Jewish Holiday Hilarity
Vol. 7 – Yiddishe Nachas

I hope you find these books entertaining and a source for sharing funny jokes, anecdotes, and incidents with your circle of family and friends. And I hope you'll continue reading the daily blog posts at www.jewishhumorcentral.com.

Al Kustanowitz
Publisher and Blogger-in-Chief
Jewish Humor Central

PART 1: JEWISH TRACES IN UNEXPECTED PLACES

AFRICA

The Igbo Jews of Nigeria

Over the years there have been reports of thousands of Africans living in Nigeria and practicing Judaism.

Several years ago, the Internet was introduced into the more rural parts of southeast Nigeria. As it has done for so many people around the world, it opened the eyes of a few young Igbo people and began answering some difficult questions of identity. For Shmuel (who was then called Sam), the nagging question he wanted answered was whether there was any truth to the long-told lore that the Igbo people were once Jews.

He began by comparing Hebrew traditions to Igbo traditions, and what he found astounded him. The similarities were so convincing that it sent him off on a journey in the quest to find other Igbo who might be practicing Judaism.

RE-EMERGING: The Jews of Nigeria is a documentary journey into the heart of Igboland and into the lives and culture of the Igbo people. The film introduces the world to the many synagogues that dot the land, and a handful of passionate, committed, and diverse characters -- each striving to fulfill their historical legacy with few resources and unbeknownst to most of the world.

Here's a preview of the film. Click on the URL to see it:

http://youtu.be/lDBowkKsGgU

Havdalah with the Orthodox Jewish Community in Uganda

Just in case you didn't know (and we didn't know either until recently) there are Orthodox Jews in Uganda.

They call themselves the *Abayudaya* of *Kahal Kadosh She'erit Yisrael* (remnants of Israel). They are a group of 129 adults and children who want to achieve a formal Orthodox conversion and immigrate to Israel.

How this community came to be is a fascinating story that began around 1917, when Semei Kakungulu, who ruled Uganda as a "warrior and governor", studied the *Tanach* and was determined to adopt an observance that was similar to those of B'nei Yisrael - The Jewish People. Formally Kakungulu was practicing a Malakite faith, a mixture of Judaism and Christianity that nowadays could be referred to as "Messianic Judaism".

However Kakungulu discarded the Christian elements of his faith after coming across a verse in Isaiah (56: 1-8) which stated that Gentiles who unite and choose to observe the Mitzvah of Hashem would be accounted a blessing. Kakungulu decided to adopt and practice only the Mitzvot (laws) written in the Tanach - the "Old Testament" - Chumash. Being very ambitious with his new unique faith, Kakungulu, his family and all his followers circumcised all their foreskins and resolved to observe the mitzvah of Brit Milah from that day onwards, a practice carried on up to this day.

You can read the whole history of this community on their website, which includes photos, videos, testimonials from visitors, and a list of their projects which include building a mikveh, starting a chicken farm, growing coffee, recording and marketing a CD of their music, and sending a member of the community to a Yeshiva in America to be trained as a rabbi.

Here is a video of the Abayudaya singing the Havdalah ceremony at the conclusion of Shabbat.

Type the URL into your browser address bar to see the video:

http://youtu.be/l8ZpGWJKBfo

A Sefer Torah Arrives in Uganda

Now that you know the story of the Abayudaya Orthodox Jews of Putti, Uganda, we're adding an update of the story with a video of the arrival of a new sefer Torah for the community.

This is a truly amazing, unbelievable but true story about how a 51-year-old Jewish spinal surgeon from Plano, Texas, was successful in getting and delivering a Torah scroll to the Abayudaya community. To get the full impact of the story, you should read the complete article from the Dallas Post and Courier.

The Abayudaya community was founded in the 1920s by Ugandan warlord Semei Kakungulu, who rejected the Christian teachings of British missionaries and converted to Judaism.

After circumcising himself and his sons and ordering his male converts to follow suit, Kakungulu compiled a book of rules and prayers for members of his tribe. In it, he demanded strict adherence to commandments in the Old Testament.

Judaism thrived in Uganda, even after Kakungulu's death in 1928. When Ugandan dictator Idi Amin came to power in 1971, he outlawed Judaism and threatened to execute anyone who practiced the religion. The decree fractured the Abayudaya and forced its most loyal adherents underground.

Freedom of religious practice was reinstated after Amin was deposed in 1979. About 1,500 Abayudaya Jews live in villages in eastern Uganda today.

Now that you know the story, watch and enjoy the video of the joyous celebration in Putti when the Torah was delivered by Dr. Lieberman.

Type the URL into your browser address bar to see the video:

http://youtu.be/R-3b7ls3-dI

Uganda Jews Sing a Song of Shalom

In 2011 we posted two videos about the Abayudaya Jewish Community of Uganda and told about their origins in 1919 and how the founder of their community embraced Judaism.

It's a fascinating story about how Judaism emerged in central Africa, complete with a Yeshiva and Beit Midrash for Torah study and traditional prayer services with tallit and tefillin. The community observes Shabbat and the laws of kashrut.

Now the Abayudaya and Israeli artist Irene Orleansky have partnered to create "Shalom, Mirembe!" as part of a music collection from Israelites and Jews of Africa and Asia.

Here is this uniquely African musical number, followed by a narrative by the spiritual leader of this community, Rabbi Gershom, of how they got started. Rabbi Gershom discusses the community's nearly 100 year history and the challenges and successes that the Abayudaya have faced during that time.

Type the URLs into your browser address bar to see the videos:

https://youtu.be/zQuoj_Yjzrs

https://youtu.be/dYAjOt46qkI

An Upside-Down Kosher L'Pesach Tombstone in Namibia

In June 2012 in the Washington Jewish Week. It was reported that in the country of Namibia, formerly called Southwest Africa, there is a tombstone in a cemetery in the capital city of Windhoek that once was engraved with the Hebrew words "Kosher L'Pesach" upside down.

This has been a sort of urban legend for the last few decades, with various versions appearing on the internet, sharing the basic story line but with conflicting details such as the name of the man who was described as Kosher L'Pesach. But out of the mists of history the true story has finally come out, thanks to Harvey Leifert, who served at the American embassy in Namibia twenty years ago, and who wrote the article in the Washington Jewish Week.

As Leifert reported in the paper,

The Jewish community was small when I lived in Windhoek, and has dwindled since, but some Jews have always lived far from the capital, in small towns and on farms. One such person was Walter Galler, a resident of Swakopmund, then a small German port on the Atlantic, up the coast from the larger and better situated British port of Walvis Bay. We know little of Galler, who was born on Aug. 8, 1888, and died on Sept. 28, 1939.

Galler was married to a non-Jewish "colored," or mixed-race, woman, and when he died, the story goes, his widow arranged for a Jewish burial in the Swakopmund Cemetery, on the edge of the Namib Desert. Mrs. Galler then ordered a simple tombstone to mark her husband's grave, and she felt it must include an acknowledgement of his Jewish faith. She somehow knew that a

Hebrew inscription was appropriate, but the only Hebrew text in her home was the certification "kasher l'Pesach," found, along with a Star of David, on the label of a bottle of wine.

Mrs. Galler apparently cut out the Hebrew words and star and handed them to the stone mason. He chiseled the letters into the tombstone, but, not knowing the Hebrew alphabet, he inscribed them upside down.

There the story might have ended, but decades later, word of a "kasher l'Pesach" tombstone in a far-off cemetery was circulating in Windhoek's Jewish community. Almost uniformly, from what I have heard, members praised Mrs. Galler for making an effort to recognize and respect her late husband's religion, regardless of the, er, unorthodox result. One day in the 1970s, however, a visiting rabbi from neighboring South Africa drove to Swakopmund and inspected the grave. He determined that the upside-down Hebrew inscription must go, and so it was done. The Star of David remains, now flanked by two blank rectangles.

But, why was the inscription excised? According to Rabbi Moshe Silberhaft, the current country communities rabbi, who was not involved in the decision, "the reason it was removed is that the gravesite was becoming a tourist attraction, and it was felt that it was 'unsettling' and disrespectful for the deceased."

Over the years, Swakopmund developed into a lovely seaside resort town, attracting both Namibian and foreign visitors. Some still find their way to the local cemetery and leave a pebble on the grave that once was kosher for Pesach.

Pirke Avot (Ethics of the Fathers) Becomes a Zulu Song

Pirke Avot, the Talmud tractate known as Ethics of the Fathers, has been translated into many languages, but it took Eliezer Auerbach, a rabbi and composer from Johannesburg, South Africa to create an arrangement of a song in the Zulu language based on a famous passage in this Talmud volume.

In Avot (2:20), it is written: *Rabbi Tarfon would say: Hayom Katzer V'hamlacha meruba (The day is short, and the work is much.).* Thuli Mazibuko translated the lyrics into Zulu..

Much of the attraction of the song is that Rabbi Eliezer Auerbach has joined with some of the best African singers in the Wits University Choir who managed to connect to the message and the values taken from Jewish sources, and transfer these through the song to the masses. The African language words fit with the rhythm and melody perfectly and a Zulu song was born.

The video below shows Rabbi Auerbach singing the song with a group of his students.

The Zulu lyrics are:
I langa I langa I langa lifisha. Nomsebenzi benzi moningi.
Basebenzi baya vilapa iholo labo labo lilingi.
I langa lifishi nomsebenzi moningi basebenzi baya vilapa iholo labo lilingi umphati uyaququzela.

Type the URL into your browser address bar to see the video:

https://youtu.be/g24pTE6a7Io

Sukkot Concert and Braai in Johannesburg, South Africa

This year Sukkot coincided with the South African public holiday, Heritage Day.

Since South Africans are encouraged to celebrate their diversity of cultures, beliefs and traditions, this was a good opportunity for one of South Africa's Jewish Outreach organizations to organize a concert of local soul and pop music talent to celebrate both religion and culture.

The educational and outreach organization Soul Workout organized the Soul Simcha concert. Amid the smoke of *braai* (barbecue) fires, performers sang in Hebrew and English. A children's choir stole the show as South Africans got an exposure to Jewish culture and music that usually appears only at weddings and bar mitzvahs.

It turned out to be a joyful family evening filled with Jewish music and *Boerewors* rolls – South Africa's version of a hotdog. The event was recorded and reported on by JN1, the Jewish-interest news channel of the European Jewish Union.

Type the URL into your browser address bar to see the video:

https://youtu.be/_5miHsUUhbI

Chabad Rabbis Defeat South Africa Ikapa Team in Soccer

A team of Chabad rabbis triumphed over the South African Ikapa Sporting Team in a World Cup soccer match in Cape Town's soccer stadium at the start of the World Cup championship games. We knew that Chabad is everywhere on the globe, but the last place we expected to see them was in the stadium, wearing their full dress soccer uniforms, full of energy, using their heads, and scoring goal after goal to win the match.

OK, so it's really a professionally done commercial for all the good work that the Lubavitchers are doing in South Africa. But it's fun to watch, so enjoy!

Type the URL into your browser address bar to see the video:

http://www.chabad.org/1242484

Making Challah in the Moroccan Mellah

In Morocco, the old Jewish Quarter is called the Mellah (Yes, the name derives from the Hebrew word for salt.) The art of braiding and baking challah is still very much alive there.

This short video shows the rolling, braiding and shaping of traditional Jewish Challah bread to the accompaniment of some lively Moroccan music. Its preparation is one of the classes offered in the Moroccan hotels that are part of the Sans Souci Collection. Now, if only they included the recipe for the dough which seems unusually pliable and easy to work with.

This was filmed in the old Jewish neighbourhood of Marrakech, where today there are only a few families that still live and preserve these traditions.

Type the URL into your browser address bar to see the video:

https://youtu.be/gUmteGA7sCg

THE AMERICAS

Black Jewish Teen Wins Irish Dancing Championship

Drew Lovejoy, a 17-year-old from rural Ohio, is not the first person you would think of as the winner of the all-Ireland dancing championship for three years in a row. To start with, he isn't Irish, he's American, with a white Jewish mother from Iowa and a black Baptist father from Georgia.

As Sabrina Tavernise wrote in the New York Times on St. Patrick's Day:

Drew is the first to admit that this is a lot to take in, so he sometimes hides part of his biography for the sake of convenience. As in 2010, when he became the first person of color to win the world championship for Irish dancing — the highest honor in that small and close-knit world — and a group of male dancers in their 70s, all of them Irish, offered their congratulations.

"They said, 'We never thought it would happen, but we're thrilled that it did,' " said Drew's mother, Andee Goldberg. She added, "They don't even know he's Jewish. That hasn't been broached. I think it would be too overwhelming."

Neither mother nor son can remember a time Drew wasn't dancing, or the reason that he started. Drew thought it might have had to do with his mother getting tired of Disney movies and playing Fred Astaire and Gene Kelly videos for him. She also took him to musicals and theater performances.

But when he went to a friend’s Irish dance competition in Indianapolis, and saw the girls and boys leaping and skipping, dancing that was part tap, part ballet set to very happy music, he was hooked.

“I was like, ‘Yeah, right,’ ” his mother said, shaking her head. “You’re biracial and you’re a Jew. We thought you had to be Irish and Catholic.”

He said, “I was like, ‘I want a medal.’ ”

And that's what he got. Here's a video clip from the local TV station in Iowa.

Type the URL into your browser address bar to see the video:

https://youtu.be/bJ9fQm2vWzM

The 99 Cent Chef Invents the Loxaco -- A Jewish Taco

Billy Vasquez, aka The 99 Cent Chef, has worked his way to the top tier of the blogosphere by removing the haute from haute cuisine. He cooks and finds interesting and tasty low-cost meals in and around Los Angeles using ingredients that cost 99 cents or less.

Well, this time he's made an exception, and used a high priced ingredient, smoked salmon, to create a new dish, the Loxaco, or Jewish taco.

Vasquez recently created the Loxaco, a Mexican twist on bagels and lox, to celebrate the opening of a lending library and used bookstore called "Libros Schmibros" in the Boyle Heights neighborhood of Los Angeles. The chef not only assembles the Loxaco, but also cures his own lox, using fresh salmon and a mixture of salt and sugar for two days in the refrigerator, before serving it in a taco.

In the last ten seconds of the video, he goes a bit too far and strays into very non-kosher territory, but otherwise, all is strictly kosher and easy for you to prepare in your own kitchen. Looks like a lighter version of the traditional bagels and lox, and it would go well with some mariachi music in the background.

Type the URL into your browser address bar to see the video:

http://youtu.be/lwwZbopLaIU

Meet Craig Cohen, the Jewish Cowboy from New Mexico

Have you heard about Craig Cohen, who calls himself the Jewish Cowboy from Rio Rancho, New Mexico, and his horse Lulu?

In the video below, Cohen says that Lulu was Horse Mitzvahed by Rabbi Arthur Flicker, a cowboy rabbi from El Paso via Columbus, Ohio, and shows us the Magen David she wears around her head.

He learned to speak horse in 2002 and shows how he communicates with Lulu by massaging her behind, and demonstrates a bit of horsemanship without actually riding Lulu, who is tethered to a tree.

Type the URL into your browser address bar to see the video:

https://vimeo.com/5795616

Latino Jews Keep Their Traditions Alive In Crown Heights

The next time you meet an immigrant from Mexico, he just might be a Lubavitcher chasid from Guadalajara, Mexico or from Argentina. Living in Crown Heights, Brooklyn, the Latino chasidim blend in with the locals. But though they look and dress like most Chasidim, they're not forsaking their Latino traditions.

Chasidic Mexican-American Jews like Moshe Nunez can flip a mean tortilla with his hands (spatulas are off limits for real Mexicans, he says) and load it up with eggs, jalapenos, and three kinds of queso (cheese).

Nunez is proud of his Mexican roots and talks about maintaining his association with Hispanic culture and his sensitivity to the plight of the *anusim* or *Marranos*, Jews in Spain who had to hide their identity for many years to avoid being forcibly converted to Christianity. In this interview on CNN, he gives a tour of his Crown Heights neighborhood and demonstrates his Latino cooking skills.

Type the URL into your browser address bar to see the video:

http://youtu.be/XvdhRra6cP8

New York City Marathon Starts With an Outdoor Minyan

For observant Jewish runners, the annual New York City Marathon starts not with the firing of a starter gun, but with the opening words of the morning prayer service.

Since 1983, Jewish runners from all levels of observance, young and old, men and women, come together before sunrise under a tent at Fort Wadsworth, Staten Island, to daven *Shacharit* with a minyan before the race begins.

Jewish Humor Central reporter and photographer Meyer Berkowitz joined the group to record the event and assist in collecting the tallitot and tefillin of the runners and delivering them to their owners at the end of the race.

The International Marathon Minyan was started in 1983 by Peter Berkowsky, an Orthodox shul-goer from New Jersey and Rabbi Jim Michaels, a marathoner rabbi from Queens who had davened alone on the parade ground the previous year.

Berkowsky had just completed a year of saying Kaddish for his mother. His primary motive was to accommodate other runners who were saying Kaddish, but over the years he realized that the morning service had evolved into something more important than just a minyan of convenience for mourners.

Berkowsky wrote a letter to a local Jewish paper asking for participants in the Marathon minyan. Rabbi Michaels responded enthusiastically, and that's how the minyan started.

The minyan benefited from the early and constant support of the late Fred Lebow, the legendary creator and promoter of the New York City Marathon, and world consultant on long-distance running.

In the minyan's third year, the organizers asked him to move the marathon from October to November to avoid a conflict with *Simchat Torah*. Lebow, a Holocaust refugee with frum roots, enthusiastically agreed, and that's where it has remained ever since.

Type the URL into your browser address bar to see the video:

https://youtu.be/DRNGNhzfvqQ

Subways are for Klezmer

An unexpected one-man klezmer concert took place in the Times Square subway station in New York.

OK, so Manhattan isn't an unexpected place to hear Jewish music. But in the subway???

There's a lot that's unknown about this episode, but we'll tell you what is self-evident from the video below. An unidentified man dressed in black tie and tails plays eight popular Jewish songs on a New York subway platform, the first three on a saxophone and the next five on a clarinet.

The songs are *Hava Nagila, Yismechu Hashamayim, Jerusalem of Gold, Eleh Chamda Libi, Bashanah Haba'ah, Mayim Mayim, Let My People Go*, and *Eliyahu Hanavi.*

This is so typical New York. The musician plays while running around a litter can in the center of the platform while the trains come and go. Most people ignore him, walking by without stopping. Occasionally, someone drops a coin or bill into his collection box while others drop garbage into the litter can.

We're lucky that at least one observer (TubeDude78, who posted it on YouTube) had a camera or phone and captured this five minute gem.

After two minutes he takes one minute off to change instruments and adjust his clarinet before continuing with the next five songs, so don't be put off by the silence between the 2 minute and 3 minute marks.

Type the URL into your browser address bar to see the video:

https://youtu.be/hgS4muofHmA

One month later, the clarinetist was revealed to be Isaiah Richardson, Jr. a very talented musician who plays venues in New York City and who posted another video clip of him playing Jewish wedding music in Central Park. Type the URL into your browser address bar to see it:

https://youtu.be/3y13sgS9yNE

Hasidic Singers Kick Off Baseball Game With National Anthems

A group of Hasidic singers took to the field last week in Coney Island to kick off the annual baseball game between the New York Police Department team and a team of players from the Flatbush Hatzolah volunteeer ambulance service of Brooklyn, New York.

At first the singers ran into difficulties with the microphone and the words, but then the leader of the group whipped out his smartphone to read the lyrics and belted out the National Anthem while the backup singers hummed along.

They followed up by singing another patriotic song, God Bless America, and this time they knew the words. We think Irving Berlin would have been proud.

P.S. As reported by The Yeshiva World News, the Hatzolah team beat the NYPD team, 8-6.

Type the URLs into your browser address bar to see the videos:

https://youtu.be/9NBegi2ozaE

https://youtu.be/7BWJpHjQ6H8

.

When Jazz Singer Billie Holliday Sang "My Yiddishe Mama"

The legendary songstress Billie Holiday, died in 1959 at the age of 44. A few years before her death, Holiday recorded an impromptu cover of the Jewish classic *My Yiddishe Mama*, which was composed by Jack Yellen and Lew Pollack and popularized by vaudeville star Sophie Tucker in 1925.

By the late 1930s, Billie Holiday had toured with Count Basie and Artie Shaw, scored a string of radio and retail hits with Teddy Wilson, and became an established artist in the recording industry. Her songs *What A Little Moonlight Can Do* and *Easy Living* were being imitated by singers across America and were quickly becoming jazz standards.[

As Elissa Goldstein wrote in Tablet Magazine,

The song has been covered many times, by everyone from the Barry Sisters to Neil Sedaka to—improbably—Tom Jones, who apparently learned it from his father, a Welsh coal miner. (Also noteworthy: a rendition by Ray Charles on the set of *The Nanny*.)

Holiday's version is something else entirely: with a simple piano accompaniment, it's nostalgic but not kitschy, full of sentiment without being sentimental, evoking both strength and vulnerability.

According to the liner notes of the Idelsohn Society's 2011 compilation "Black Sabbath: The Secret Musical History of Black-Jewish Relations," the song was recorded at the New York City home of clarinetist Tony Scott, in an effort to coax his baby into 'talking' into the microphone.

Another version of the story, by musician Jack Gottlieb, has it that the child was the son of William Dufty, who co-authored Holiday's autobiography, "Lady Sings the Blues." In any event, Holiday's crooning is successful—how could it fail?—and the child can be heard cooing toward the end of the recording. It's a delightful, candid moment.

Type the URL into your browser address bar to see the video:

https://youtu.be/Dowy5Jdb-Yg

African-American Convert Embraces Yiddish Music

New Yiddish singing stars are hard to find these days. Yiddish songs are usually sung by veterans of the old Second Avenue Yiddish theatre circuit and in revivals by theatre groups such as the Folksbiene Playhouse.

Now a new, dynamic opera singer, Anthony Russell, has emerged on the Yiddish singing scene. An African-American from a devout Christian family who became enamored with Judaism and Yiddish, Russell has embraced his new religion and the music that gives expression to it.
As Renee Ghert-Zand wrote in The Times of Israel,

If you think you know what a Yiddish singing star looks like, think again. The new, hot name in the world of Yiddish musical performance is Anthony Russell, and he's a 33-year-old, 6'1" African-American hipster from Oakland, California. Russell, whose full stage name is Anthony Mordechai Tzvi Russell, is a Jew by choice, an opera singer by training, and a Yiddish singer by calling.

Proving that you don't need to have roots in the shtetls of Eastern Europe to connect deeply with *mammeloshen*, Russell is quickly gaining notice for his expressive interpretation of Yiddish folk songs and Hassidic *niggunim* (wordless melodies).

In this interview, Russell describes his love of all things Jewish, especially Yiddish song, and gives us a few snippets from his Yiddish repertoire.

Type the URL into your browser address bar to see the video:

https://youtu.be/N_eGpHqTmNg

Yiddish Thrives at the University of Texas

Yiddish 101 is an introduction to an ancient language that's attracting new interest at the University of Texas. Richard Schlesinger has a video report on the Austin classroom where conversations sound like they could be taking place at a Hasidic Jewish bakery in Williamsburg, Brooklyn.

This video was shown on the CBS Sunday Morning TV show last week. It focuses on the resurgence of spoken Yiddish in Texas classrooms. The report includes comments by a University of Texas Vietnamese student who is adding Yiddish to her language repertory, a visit to the National Yiddish Book Center in Amherst, Massachusetts and its founder Aaron Lansky, and to the streets of Williamsburg where Yiddish is the main spoken language of its Hasidic residents.

We also get a glimpse of activities of the National Center for Yiddish Film, the National Yiddish Theatre-Folksbiene, and the Klezmatics, one of the oldest bands playing the Klezmer music that was the dominant musical form in Eastern Europe.

Type the URL into your browser address bar to see the video:

https://youtu.be/_eMybmNfIYg

Yiddish Tango is Fusion of Klezmer and Argentinian Tango

The Argentinian Tango emerged from the slums of Buenos Aires, but over the years it absorbed other musical strains as immigrants from other countries came to Argentina.

Jews from Eastern Europe have been immigrating to Argentina and they brought with them klezmer music that has fused with the tango to create a unique music and dance form...the Yiddish Tango.

As Elizabeth Lee writes in The Jewish Voice,

For Argentine-born Gustavo Bulgach, tango is music with an attitude.
"Tango means the blues. Tango is not just tango - it means - it's an attitude that you want to express. In every language, in Yiddish, in Spanish - in whatever language - Tango represents that kind of attitude of losing or having your heart broken by life," Bulgach says.

"Tango is not only Argentinian. It's a loop from Europe also. It's like something dramatic, and it's the count...maybe one, two, three," says vocalist Divina Gloria.

The band pays tribute to the music of the Jewish immigrants in Argentina. Bulgach is Jewish, and his family emigrated to Argentina from Russia. Jewish vocalist Divina Gloria's family came from Poland. Yiddish tango evokes memories of her own childhood in Argentina.

Type the URL into your browser address bar to see the video:

https://youtu.be/R8IwUEy61KM

Israeli Dance Flourishes With a Mexican Twist

In 1971, Carlos Halpert organized a group of young Mexican artists, creating an interdisciplinary, traditional Jewish dance group called *Anajnu Veatem* (*Anachnu v'Atem* - We and You.)

The group integrates Israeli and Mexican music and dance, linking traditional folklore and contemporary Jewish and Mexican themes.

They have toured almost all the states in the Mexican Republic and some cities in other countries, performing in theaters, open air stages, festivals, concerts in cultural institutions, universities, public plazas, social centers, and regional fairs.

Anajnu v'Atem have performed their signature piece, *Un Poco de lo Nuestro*, in many venues, including Mexico City's Palace of Fine Arts. It's a beautiful blend of Mexican and Israeli musical and dance styles, a melange of Tzena Tzena, Hava Nagila, BaShana HaBa'ah, Dovid Melech Yisrael, and Hevenu Shalom Aleichem.

Type the URL into your browser address bar to see the video:

http://youtu.be/T5y8oWpVrkg

A Mystery in Mexico

The state of Coahuila, in northern Mexico, shares a border, the Rio Grande, with Texas. It has been reported over the years that *Anusim*, secret Jews who escaped from the Spanish Inquisition, traveled to Mexico and settled there.

A university in Coahuila staged an arts festival that included 15 minutes of Hebrew music and dance. The video, which is posted below, left us somewhat confused. We enjoy digging up back stories for most of our blog posts, but for this one, the back story eludes us.

So what's the mystery? The dances are Israeli, but the dancers appear to be Mexican. The boys wear kippot and a few wear tzitzit, but their shirts look very much like those worn by Messianic Christian groups in Central and South America who have an affinity for Israeli dancing. Some of the T-shirts feature the Hebrew word *tekuma* in large type. The word can be translated as reistance, revival, rebirth, or resurrection. A man wrapped in a tallit blows a Yemenite shofar at seemingly random places in the midst of the dancing and singing. And about 5 minutes into the set, they start to dance an Italian tarantella.

Type the URL into your browser address bar to see the video:

https://youtu.be/KU4LP_s_pTo

Moses Parts Traffic and Spilled Coca-Cola in Film Festival

Jewish Film Festivals are popping up all over the world. Just about every major city, and some minor ones, are presenting new films to eager audiences. In reviewing lists of the films that are being shown, we noticed that most explore serious themes, and very few are true comedies. When we find a comedy, we try to bring it to your attention.

The lack of comedy in Jewish film doesn't stop the festival promoters from indulging in humor, sometimes irreverent, in calling attention to the festivals themselves.

The scene of Charlton Heston as Moses parting the Red Sea in Cecil B. DeMille's *The Ten Commandments* was just too powerful an image not to inspire comedic copying in commercials for Jewish Film Festivals in Mexico and Canada.

In the first clip below, a couple is driving through busy Mexico City traffic, trying to get to a movie theater before the film starts. When traffic comes to a standstill, they despair and ask for a miracle.

Moses appears atop a van in full DeMille regalia, raises his arms and extends his staff. The cars split into two rows, allowing the couple's car to pass through.

In the second clip, a couple buys a large cola at a movie theater concession stand, and the guy spills it all on the floor. Enter Moses, actually a janitor with a mop, who raises his arms and with a mighty roar splits the cola puddle and lets the girl pass through on dry land.

When she passes through, the Moses character lowers his arms. Her date tries to follow her, but fails as the cola spill returns to its original form as the Moses character says "Loser!"

Type the URLs into your browser address bar to see the videos:

https://youtu.be/2xCWATTz8eI

https://youtu.be/lgbtS-SFUmU

ASIA AND AUSTRALIA

Japanese Hebrew Choir in Sings in Kyoto

Last week's post of a Chinese chorus singing Yiddish and Hebrew songs in Hong Kong got such a positive response that we just had to share the songs of another choir 1,500 miles across the East China Sea in Kyoto, Japan.

We don't know if the choir of Beit Shalom in Kyoto sings in Yiddish, but their Hebrew singing is beautiful. Beit Shalom (House of Peace) is the headquarters of the Japanese Christian Friends of Israel. The group is well known for its choir, the Shinome (Dawn) Chorus, which sings Israeli and Japanese songs and has traveled to Israel, Europe, and the United States. The group's main ideology centers on support for Israel and includes prayers for the coming of the Messiah.

Rather than encourage conversion to Christianity, the group emphasizes peace between peoples. Ehud Olmert visited Beit Shalom when he was the mayor of Jerusalem. Jews and Israelis are specifically welcome to stay at Beit Shalom for up to three nights free of charge.

In this video, the Beit Shalom choir sings *Lalechet Shevi Acharaich*, an Israeli song by Ehud Manor made popular by the singer Ilanit, *Ohr*, and *Yerushalayim Shel Zahav* (Jerusalem of Gold).

Type the URL into your browser address bar to see the video:

https://youtu.be/fEHMOz92cok

Are the Japanese the Ten Lost Tribes of Israel?

Sometimes it seems like everyone is looking for the Ten Lost Tribes of Israel. Every few years a story pops up of the exiled ten northern tribes actually being in India, Myanmar, China, or Korea.

The idea that somehow the missing tribes found their way along the Silk Road to Japan has been proposed more than a few times, and teams of scholars and archaeologists have studied the possibility over the years.

Lately there has been a proliferation of videos on the internet which claim to provide evidence that these stories are not myths, but realities. The evidence offered includes similarities in ways that festivals and prayer are observed, in symbols that seem identical or close approximations, and in words and phrases in Hebrew and Japanese that are remarkably alike.

We'll share a video with you and let you be the judge. It focuses on similarity of rituals and festivals including "Japanese tefilin" and a Rosh Chodesh festival.

Is this Jewish-Japanese connection a real possibility or just a fantasy? Watch the video and decide.

Type the URL into your browser address bar to see the video:

http://youtu.be/4HF2FkRE-PU

Gut Shabbes Vietnam: Looking For Jews in Ho Chi Minh City

We recently found a 52 minute uplifting documentary film that is making the rounds of Jewish Film Festivals around the country. A clash of cultures and a smile of recognition are at its core. A young Israeli couple set out to the Far East – not an unusual occurrence in contemporary Israeli reality. But this couple and their baby are no ordinary pair. They are emissaries of the Chabad Movement who are sent to Vietnam - on a one-way ticket- to encourage and create a Jewish community there.

The encounter with the frantic and exuberant life in Ho Chi Minh City is a source for much confusion and amusement. The search for a real Jewish community in Vietnam is also a point of contention – as they soon discover that the local Jews are only marginally interested in a Jewish connection and many of them are married to locals.

In the face of much uncertainty Rabbi Menachem and Racheli Hartman are able to overcome their apprehension toward their foreign environment because of a deep belief in the magnitude of their mission. And so their meeting with a new and strange culture challenges them in ways that are both touching and baffling.

Menachem and Racheli arrive in Vietnam in the weeks leading up to Rosh Hashanah – the Jewish New Year. Frantic to have everything set up before the holiday begins; the couple embarks on an anxious journey to acquaint themselves with the local customs, while maintaining their own strict adherence to Jewish law.

One of their chief challenges is finding the local Jews and persuading them to then attend religious services. The Jewish community in Vietnam is an eclectic mixture of ex-Israelis and Jews from other parts of the world who have little identification with their heritage. And so - as their worried families back home follow their acclimation from a far – Racheli and Menachem undertake the work of "bringing the Messiah."

Click on the URL to see a video clip from the film:

http://youtu.be/NBoXmkHoBho

Chinese Jews Return to Israel

The first Jews arrived in Kaifeng, one of the capitals of imperial China, over a thousand years ago, when Jewish merchants from Persia settled in the area.

At its height, in the Middle Ages, Kaifeng's Jewish community numbered as many as 5,000 people, with rabbis, synagogues and various communal institutions.

But assimilation eventually began to take its toll. The last rabbi of Kaifeng died two centuries ago, and by the middle of the 19th century, the community was forced to sell the synagogue, Torah scrolls and its other remaining assets.

Until today, however, there are between 500 and 1,000 identifiable descendants of the Jewish community, and in recent years an awakening has been taking place among them, as increasing numbers of young Kaifeng Jews seek to reclaim their heritage.

In October 2009, seven young men making aliyah were interviewed at Ben Gurion airport together with three of their friends who made aliyah four years earlier. These descendants of the Kaifeng Jewish community were helped in finding their new home in Israel by *Shavei Yisrael*, an organization that strives to extend a helping hand to all members of the extended Jewish family and to all who seek to rediscover or renew their link with the people of Israel.

Type the URL into your browser address bar to see the video:

http://youtu.be/McZIVO3oliI

Zum Gali Gali, Hora Song, Gets a New Life in Korea

It's been awhile since we heard the old Israeli pioneer song, *Zum Gali Gali*. Most likely it was when our kids were singing and dancing at the *Zimriah* and *Rikudiah* at Camp Ramah in the 1980s.

But it's resurfaced in Korea. No, we're not kidding. We found it on YouTube the same day we were reading an article by Lenore Skenazy in The Forward about the decline in teaching Israeli dance at schools and camps.

In this video the Goyang Civic Choir of South Korea is not dancing the hora, but they're singing *Zum Gali Gali* in a medley of Hora songs, including *Rad HaLaila*.

At first we thought they were singing in Korean, but after listening a few times, we're pretty sure that they're singing in English, with a Korean accent.

Type the URL into your browser address bar to see the video:

http://youtu.be/5WbQ2QrlEGY

Papua New Guinea Natives Sing Sh'ma Yisrael

While these are not exactly Jewish tribesmen singing *Sh'ma Yisrael* in Hebrew in Papua New Guinea (they're tribesmen taught by Christian missionaries), we thought this video would be an interesting addition to our collection of Jewish Traces in Unexpected Places.

Papua New Guinea has been associated with mudmen, cannibals, and headhunters for many years, but we understand that these practices have been practically eliminated there. Still, a large majority of the residents are illiterate.

A Jewish convert to Christianity evidently remembered the words and melody of *Sh'ma Yisrael* and the sentence *Baruch Shem K'vod Malchuto L'olam Va'ed* and taught them to the members of this picturesque group, who repeated them with relish.

Type the URL into your browser address bar to see the video:

http://youtu.be/Go2addQMDYA

Are the Gogodala of Papua New Guinea a Lost Tribe of Israel?

Papua New Guinea is about as far from civilization as you can get. And yet members of the Gogodala tribe in that distant island insist that they are descendants of one of the ten lost tribes of Israel.

Florida International University Religious Studies Professor Tudor Parfitt visited the Gogodala people of Papua New Guinea, a tribe of former headhunters who claim to be one of the Lost Tribes of Israel.

Back in 2011 we posted a video of Papua New Guinea tribesmen reciting the Sh'ma Yisrael prayer.

The leaders of the tribe say their ancestors told them that they came to Papua New Guinea from Jerusalem in canoes. So far the DNA tests conducted by the FIU professor have beeen inconclusive, neither confirming or denying their identity claim.

Type the URL into your browser address bar to see the video:

https://youtu.be/ioFpk_8iY5M

The Tribe of Menashe, a Lost Tribe of Israel, Returns

The Bnei Menashe (sons of Manasseh) claim descent from one of the Ten Lost Tribes of Israel, who were sent into exile by the Assyrian Empire more than 27 centuries ago.

Their ancestors wandered through Central Asia and the Far East for centuries, before settling in what is now northeastern India, along the border with Burma and Bangladesh.

Throughout their sojourn in exile, the Bnei Menashe continued to practice Judaism just as their ancestors did, including observing the Sabbath, keeping kosher, celebrating the festivals and following the laws of family purity. And they continued to nourish the dream of one day returning to the land of their ancestors, the Land of Israel.

In recent years, Shavei Israel has brought some 1,700 Bnei Menashe back home to Zion. Another 7,200 still remain in India, waiting for the day when they too will be able to return to Israel and the Jewish people.

The video below shows scenes of the Bnei Menashe arriving at Ben-Gurion airport in Tel Aviv and their daily activities in communities around Israel.

Type the URL into your browser address bar to see the video:

https://youtu.be/DutFZ9abLH0

An American Jewish Comedian Visits the Jews of India

Entwine is an initiative of the American Jewish Joint Distribution Committee, commonly known as "the Joint." It's a movement for young Jewish leaders and offers them service experiences in Jewish communities around the world.

The JDC is the world's leading Jewish humanitarian assistance organization. It works in more than 70 countries and in Israel to alleviate hunger and hardship, rescue Jews in danger, create lasting connections to Jewish life, and provide immediate relief and long-term development support for victims of natural and man-made disasters.

Entwine sent American comedian Noah Gardenswartz to India to meet the local Jewish community. They asked him to film everything. In today's video, we follow Noah to Mumbai and Cochin and share his experiences.

Type the URL into your browser address bar to see the video:

https://youtu.be/DLis4Cnepo8

A Tiny Spark Flickers in Indonesia

Indonesia is one of the last places you'd expect to find a Jewish community. But there is one, in Manado, one of the most remote cities in the far-flung country, and it's hanging on, but just barely.

The New York Times ran an article describing how a tiny spark of Judaism is flickering in Manado, a small city that's always been more tolerant of minorities than Indonesia's more populated cities. The article is worth reading because it shows how the efforts of a few dedicated people are changing attitudes in the country with the largest Muslim population in the world.

How are a few families who embraced the faith of their Dutch Jewish ancestors making their presence felt in Indonesia? By forming a very unusual coalition -- with a local legislator, tourism advocates, evangelical Christians, and a Chabad rabbi from Singapore, about 1500 miles away.

As Norimitsu Onishi reported in The New York Times,

A new, 62-foot-tall menorah, possibly the world's largest, rises from a mountain overlooking this Indonesian city, courtesy of the local government. Flags of Israel can be spotted on motorcycle taxi stands, one near a six-year-old synagogue that has received a face-lift, including a ceiling with a large Star of David, paid for by local officials.

Long known as a Christian stronghold and more recently as home to evangelical and charismatic Christian groups, this area on the fringes of northern Indonesia has become the unlikely setting for increasingly public displays of pro-Jewish sentiments as some people have embraced the faith of their Dutch Jewish ancestors. With the local governments' blessing, they are carving out a small space for themselves in the sometimes strangely shifting religious landscape of Indonesia, the country with the world's largest Muslim population.

Jewish music has somehow found its way into this country, and we bring you an example in this video of Indonesians singing *Hevenu Shalom Aleichem*. But that's only the first three minutes of the video. Go any further and you'll find yourself in the middle of Christmas music.

Type the URL into your browser address bar to see the video:

http://youtu.be/3SsXjf4xADY

Looking For a Jewish Husband in Sexy Beijing

Anna Sophie Loewenberg has traveled very far in her quest to find a husband, preferably Jewish. The Los Angeles born Loewenberg, 36, lives and works in Beijing, China, and has been producing, writing and starring in an internet program, *Sexy Beijing*, depicting her adventures as she looks for love in China's capital city.

As Sharon Usadin wrote in The Jewish Week,

Loewenberg goes by the more pronounceable Chinese name of "Su Fei," despite its double meaning as a brand of Chinese maxi-pads. Her shtick – with nearly 3.6 million YouTube hits – has landed her in English-language Chinese papers, on the Today Show and even in a Q&A on The New Yorker's Web site.

After growing up in California hearing stories about her grandparents' and father's escape from Nazi Europe to Shanghai, Loewenberg finally decided to move to China herself in 1996 with a teaching program, where she also learned to speak fluent Mandarin and eventually began working as a journalist.

"It was always just part of the story of my family growing up," Loewenberg said. "There were always these books of photographs there in our living room. But I never got to meet my grandparents, so it didn't seem real almost."

She left China in 2001 to attend Columbia University's School of Journalism in New York, but found herself back in Beijing by 2006, working on a documentary film business called Danwei TV with two of her friends, Luke Mines and Jeremy Goldkorn. Only after she resettled in the city, Loewenberg said, did the concept for "Sexy

Beijing" materialize.

The show opens very similarly to HBO's "Sex and the City," with the camera spinning over tower cranes atop half-built Beijing high-rises, rather than Manhattan's glamorous Empire State building. Instead of getting splashed by a New York City bus a la Carrie, Su Fei falls victim to a bombardment of bikers, a rolling dumpster and a stray watering hose. Wearing her signature horn-rimmed glasses, Su Fei types stories on her Macbook in between scenes, interjecting voiceover words of wisdom.

In this episode, Su Fei attends the opening of the new mikveh at Beijing's Chabad House, gets a lesson in family purity from the local Chabadniks, and learns why she can't take advantage of the luxurious facilities.

Type the URL into your browser address bar to see the video:

http://youtu.be/Wp2tyCiDTGg

Chinese Chorus Sings in Yiddish and Hebrew

Would you expect a Chinese Chorus to sing the Yiddish song *Oifn Pripitchik* and the Hebrew song *Yerushalayim Shel Zahav*? Well, Jewish traces show up in the most unlikely places, and Hong Kong is no exception.

The Chinese University of Hong Kong Student Chorus performs the music of many cultures in many languages, and Yiddish and Hebrew are part of their repertoire. They also sing in Finnish, Japanese, German and Latin.

The video we're sharing today is titled *Choral Selections from Schindler's List*. We had forgotten that these two songs were included in the Steven Spielberg film. But here they are, preceded by a violinist playing the plaintive theme from the movie, with which he also closes the medley.

Type the URL into your browser address bar to see the video:

https://youtu.be/3WAImK9FPDs

Taiwan University Chorus Performs "Fiddler on the Roof"

This has been quite a year for *Fiddler on the Roof.* After celebrating its 50th anniversary in June 2014, a major revival was launched in December 2015 at the Broadway Theatre in New York City.

The new production, highly acclaimed in reviews in The New York Times and other publications, is stimulating new interest around the world in what has become a classic and universal story.

Another 50th anniversary was celebrated just a year earlier in Taiwan, where the National Taiwan University Chorus marked 50 years on campus. The chorus consists of around 100 avid choral singers, none of whom are music majors.

Bright and youthful, with promising potential and remarkably adaptable talent, singers of NTU Chorus delight in performing works from a wide range of choral repertoire, including canonic Western choral works, spirituals and gospel music, Chinese art songs, Taiwanese folksongs, operatic choral numbers, musical medleys, and commissioned works by Taiwan's own emerging talented composers.

Last week they performed a 25 minute long concert version of Fiddler on the Roof that we hope you will enjoy.

Type the URL into your browser address bar to see the video:

https://youtu.be/SXkHoFAg4vA

Japanese Hebrew Choir in Kyoto

Our post of a Chinese chorus singing Yiddish and Hebrew songs in Hong Kong got such a positive response that we just had to share the songs of another choir 1,500 miles across the East China Sea in Kyoto, Japan.

We don't know if the choir of Beit Shalom in Kyoto sings in Yiddish, but their Hebrew singing is beautiful. Beit Shalom (House of Peace) is the headquarters of the Japanese Christian Friends of Israel. The group is well known for its choir, the Shinome (Dawn) Chorus, which sings Israeli and Japanese songs and has traveled to Israel, Europe, and the United States. The group's main ideology centers on support for Israel and includes prayers for the coming of the Messiah.

Rather than encourage conversion to Christianity, the group emphasizes peace between peoples. Ehud Olmert visited Beit Shalom when he was the mayor of Jerusalem. Jews and Israelis are specifically welcome to stay at Beit Shalom for up to three nights free of charge.

In this video, the Beit Shalom choir sings *Lalechet Shevi Acharaich*, an Israeli song by Ehud Manor made popular by the singer Ilanit, *Or*, and *Yerushalayim Shel Zahav* (Jerusalem of Gold).

Type the URL into your browser address bar to see the video:

https://youtu.be/fEHMOz92cok

Fiddler on the Roof's "To Life" Works in Japanese, Too

They had us at *Sharom*! The Japanized greeting expressed with a handshake between Tevye and Lazar Wolf in this video signaled that this would be no ordinary production of *Fiddler on the Roof.*

That's the only word we recognized in the Japanese version of *L'Chayim! To Life!* from *Fiddler on the Roof.* We knew that the show had been produced in Hebrew, Yiddish, French, and Spanish, but Japanese? It turns out that cultural similarities made the show resonate with audiences in Japan.

As Miri Ben-Shalom wrote in *All About Jewish Theatre News,*

Fiddler on the Roof is a timeless hit because it appeals to everyone, everywhere – not only to Jewish audiences. It is reflected in Stewart Lane's anecdote: "When the first Japanese production of Fiddler was produced, the composers Harnick, Bock and Stein went to Japan. They were all very nervous.

'How's a New York interpretive Jewish musical is going to work in Japan? During production they are all anxiously biting their nails. At the end the Japanese producer comes over to them and says: I don't understand, I don't know how this piece can work so well in New York. It's so Japanese!"

Type the URL into your browser address bar to see the video:

https://youtu.be/XIJcaJxuOgc

A Rosh Hashanah "Cheerleader" Parody from Singapore

What song drew the most cheers this summer? OMI's *Cheerleader*, as the Jamaican reggae/pop artist's smash hit was voted *Billboard*'s No. 1 song of the summer of 2015.

The buoyant single headed *Billboard*'s annual Songs of the Summer chart, which tracks the most popular hits based on cumulative performance on the weekly Billboard Hot 100 chart from Memorial Day through Labor Day.

So what does this have to do with Rosh Hashanah? The United Hebrew Congregation of Singapore created a music video called *Sound a Tekiah*, a parody of *Cheerleader*, in which their members dance their way around the island.

There have been Jews and Orthodox synagogues in Singapore since the 1840s, but Reform Judaism did not make an appearance until 1991, when a small group of expatriate Jews founded The United Hebrew Congregation. It is made up of a Jewish Diaspora of many nationalities of Reform, Conservative, Progressive and Reconstructionist backgrounds.

Type the URL into your browser address bar to see the video:

https://youtu.be/BGTS9TVU0S0

The Talmud is a Best-Seller in South Korea

Recently The New Yorker published a fascinating article about the Talmud being a best-seller in South Korea, finding a place in most homes.

According to the author, Ross Arbes, who studied the Talmud in a day school in Atlanta, the Talmud's presence in Korea is attributable to Marvin Tokayer, a 78-year-old rabbi who lives in Great Neck, New York.

In 1962, Rabbi Tokayer served as an Air Force chaplain in Japan and South Korea, and returned to Tokyo in 1968 as the rabbi of the Jewish Community of Japan.

In the June 23, 2015 issue of The New Yorker, Arbes writes:

In 2011, the South Korean Ambassador to Israel at the time, Young-sam Ma, was interviewed on the Israeli public-television show "Culture Today." "I wanted to show you this," he told the host, straying briefly from the topic at hand, a Korean film showing in Tel Aviv.

It was a white paperback book with "Talmud" written in Korean and English on the cover, along with a cartoon sketch of a Biblical character with a robe and staff. "Each Korean family has at least one copy of the Talmud. Korean mothers want to know how so many Jewish people became geniuses."

Looking up at the surprised host, he added, "Twenty-three per cent of Nobel Prize winners are Jewish people. Korean women want to know the secret. They found the secret in this book."

Mincha and Shabtai Zvi in Turkey

Continuing our series of Jewish observance and culture in countries where it's least expected, the Forward's Yiddish language reporter, Itzik Gottesman, narrates a travelogue of a family vacation in Turkey. The narration is in Yiddish, with full English subtitles.

The trip includes Istanbul and Izmir, where they encounter Sephardic Jews looking for a minyan in an abandoned Ashkenazi Synagogue. Gottesman joins the minyan and gets a tour of a few Sephardic synagogues, guided by the Ladino-speaking gabbai.

Afterward, they look for and find the home of Shabtai Zvi, the false messiah who later converted to Islam to the great disappointment of his followers. The bottom line: Turkey is a great place to visit, and they had no fear of being Jews in a Muslim country.

Type the URL into your browser address bar to see the video:
http://youtu.be/z-_VJpEz7Fk

The Mountain Jews of Azerbaijan

During the past two years we have profiled Jewish life in unexpected places in the world: Uganda, Indonesia, Guatemala, Beijing, Vietnam, and Japan. Now we have come across a community of Jews living in the mountainous regions of Azerbaijan and Dagestan.

As Kevin Gould reported in the London Jewish Chronicle,

Gyrmyzy Gasaba (in Russian, Krasnaya Sloboda or "Red Roofs") is perhaps the world's only all-Jewish town outside Israel. It sits across the Gudialcay River from the Muslim town of Guba. Where Guba seems poor and perhaps a little care-worn, Gyrmyzy Gasaba appears to be prosperous and thriving - 3,600 mountain Jews live here, wearing their Judaism with pride, and without fear. Boys wearing kippot on their heads bustle about, and each house displays at least one large Magen David.

Azerbaijan is proud of its tolerance towards minorities. The national religion is Shia Islam, but Azerbaijanis are scorned by their Iranian neighbors to the south as bad, lax Muslims. That Azerbaijan enjoys friendly relations with Israel seems only to prove the Iranian point.

The Jews of Azerbaijan speak Juwuro-Tat, a language based on ancient Persian, then seasoned with Aramaic, Arabic and Hebrew.

There are many theories as to who the mountain Jews are, and how they came to be here. One suggests that they are descended from the Khazars (unlikely - the Khazars came later), another that they are ethnic Persian Tats converted to Judaism; some ethnologists regard Tats as mountain Jews converted to Islam.

Outside the yeshiva, Rav Adam subscribes to none of these schools. "Our people came here from southern Persia around 720 BCE," he says, slowly. "It seems there were some upheavals in what is now southern Iran and Iraq. We were Jewish military colonists loyal to Parthian and Sassanid rulers, sent here to the Caucasus to guard against Mongol invasions from the Pontic steppe."

Mountain Jews settled the eastern Caucasus in towns all over Dagestan, Chechniya and Azerbaijan. "There were times we were persecuted, and times of peace," says Rav Adam. "Arabs came in the 8th century, and there were forced conversions..." The Safavid ruler Nadir Shah was especially cruel, but following medical intervention by a Jewish doctor who saved his son's life, Fatali, the Khan of Guba, granted the mountain Jews sanctuary in his lands. Thus, in 1742, Gyrmyzy Gasaba was formally established. "It was known then - and now - as 'Little Jerusalem ' and as a center for Torah learning," explains Rav Adam.

In 1917 there were 18,000 Jews in Azerbaijan, but Soviet persecution and attendant famines caused many thousands to flee to Baku, Azerbaijan's capital, and beyond. Between 1979 and 1990 many of these moved to Israel, and some to Russia and the United States. Prosperity followed, and in recent times mountain Jew oligarchs Telman Ismailov and Irmik Abayev have been energetically supporting the rebirth and growth of Gyrmyzy Gasaba. As well as owning local property, retail businesses and agricultural land, mountain Jews are also instrumental in the financial and oil services industries in Baku. Rabbi Elezar is proud to relate that his community now has two shuls, 30 boys and 20 girls studying at the yeshiva, and a mikvah.

Oligarchical and community support is especially evident a five-minute drive away, where finishing touches are being put to the Bet

Knesset synagogue, which has air conditioning, and a lighthouse-like roof light from which a huge menorah beams out in all directions. The Azerbaijani taste is for ornamented zinc roofs, and in Gyrmyzy Gasaba this takes the form of metal Magen Davids that sprout everywhere above downpipes, on ceiling overhangs, and in the eaves of the well-kept houses, shops and banqueting suites.

In this video report from Jerusalem Online, you can get a closer look at the mountain Jews as they go about their daily life.

Type the URL into your browser address bar to see the video:

http://youtu.be/diOSrb911Kw

Skateboarding Rabbi Teaches Kabbalah Down Under

They don't teach it in rabbinical seminaries, but Rabbi Dovid Tsap has found a pathway to spirituality and to reaching young people in Melbourne, Australia. It's skateboarding. No, we're not kidding.

As Shane Scanlan wrote in the Docklands (Australia) News:

Rabbi Tsap, 34, is a mystic who spends his intellectual energy exploring the "more conspicuously spiritual side of Judaism".

He writes a blog called Spiritual Skateboarding and communicates his thinking with people from all over the world. And he has recently published a book exploring the depths of Kabbalah.

Being a skateboarder has dual benefits for Rabbi Tsap. Apart from the health and wellbeing benefits he derives from the demanding sport, he clearly opens a respectful channel of communication with young people.

"The kids have some degree of admiration for me and pay attention to what I say," he said. "They think of me as a friend. There is affinity and rapport."

And while he has been a Rabbi for many years, he has only been the "Skating Rabbi" in recent times. Rabbi Tsap explained that he skated as a kid but gave it up when he was 15 years old.

He was encouraged by his friend Raph Brous to get back into skateboarding less than two years ago. Since then he has seen the barriers between himself and young people diminish drastically.

"It was almost like they had too much reverence for me then," he said. "It was a barrier to effective communication."

He said it was now very easy to speak with young people about life, drugs and God.

“At last now I am starting to feel like a real rabbi,” he said.

Here's a video of Rabbi Tsap in action as reported by Australia's JNTV News. Enjoy!

Type the URL into your browser address bar to see the video:

http://youtu.be/ToaLUubBROg

EUROPE

Moscow's Turetsky Choir Brings Jewish Music to World Stages

In 1989 Michael Turetsky organized the male choir of the Moscow Synagogue. One year later, the choir made its debut in the Philharmonic Halls of Tallinn and Kaliningrad.

The Turetsky Choir has since performed on many famous stages around the world, including the Great Hall of the Moscow State Conservatory, the Kremlin Palace, the Bolshoy Theatre, Carnegie Hall, (New York) Merkin Concert Hall (New York) Jordan Hall of the Boston Conservatory, Gala Tarbut, Teatron Jerusalem (Israel), King's Palace (Madrid, Spain), in the buildings of the United Nations, and Congress (Washington, DC).

The choir's repertoire includes performances of classical, Broadway, and pop music, but Turetsky has a special affinity for Jewish and Israeli music. Here is a stirring medley of popular Jewish and Israeli music called Кошерное попурри (kosher potpourri) that the choir performed recently in a Russian concert hall.

Type the URL into your browser address bar to see the video:

http://youtu.be/5h1cPdbdZfw

Vienna Hosts First European Jewish Choir Festival

Hundreds of singers from across Europe convened in Vienna on the banks of the river Danube for the first European Jewish Choir Festival. The festival culminated last Sunday in a gala concert titled "Shir LaShalom - A Song for Peace" at the Austria Center Vienna, where 400 vocalists from Jewish choirs from 16 European cities presented their repertoires.

The event, which drew some 1,500 spectators over the weekend, was sponsored by the European Jewish Parliament, the European Jewish Union, the Jewish Community of Vienna and the Austrian state.

In addition to concerts, the festival's Jewish and non-Jewish singers participated in workshops to increase cultural exchange, an element which Roman Grinberg, choirmaster of the Vienna Jewish Choir, described as "extremely important" for organizers.

"The excitement here is enormous, and it shows in the beaming faces of participants," said Joel Rubinfeld, co-chair of the European Jewish Parliament.Rubinfeld said singers and musicians from the festival turned an informal dinner on Thursday at Vienna's Alef Alef kosher restaurant into an impromptu klezmer and song concert.

The event is to become an annual festival. Next year's gathering is scheduled to take place in Rome and, the following year, in Paris.

Type the URL into your browser address bar to see the video:

https://youtu.be/AWSVmgaJt_s

Jewish Song and Dance Returns to Belarus

Jewish life is returning to Belarus and its capital, Minsk. After the founding of yeshivot in Volozhin and Mir in the nineteenth century, the Jewish population rose to almost a million in the 1900s.

After the Holocaust, only ten percent remained, many of whom moved to Israel. Recent surveys estimate the population now to be around 50,000.

Belarus was home to many notable Jews, including Shimon Peres, Chaim Weitzman, Menachem Begin, Yitzchak Shamir, Eliezer Ben Yehuda, Rabbi Joseph B. Soloveitchik, Irving Berlin, Marc Chagall, Louis B. Mayer, David Sarnoff, and Ayn Rand.

Jewish organizations are taking root in Belarus, such as community centers, youth organizations, kindergartens, newspapers, magazines, and a web site.

A visible sign of a Jewish awakening is the performance of Jewish music in public places. In our ongoing search for new and unusual interpretations of *Tumbalalaika, Hava Nagila*, and *Hevenu Shalom Aleichem* around the world, we came across the Radzimichy Folk Ensemble of Belarus. In the video below, they sing and dance to the melodies of all three songs, dressed in their traditional folk costumes.

Type the URL into your browser address bar to see the video:

https://youtu.be/zRzO5Rn6kmU

Sharon Brauner Gives Yiddish a New Look in Berlin

Berlin isn't the first place that comes to mind when thinking about Yiddish cabaret. And isn't a Yiddish nightclub act an oxymoron, at least in today's world?

But Yiddish nightlife in Berlin is hopping, and Sharon Brauner deserves a lot of the credit for these Jewish traces in an unexpected place.

Born in West Berlin in 1969, she attended a musical school and took a job as a bouncer, bartender, and go-go dancer in Berlin's trendy clubs. Then she studied acting at the Lee Strasberg institute in New York while singing jazz standards at night in various clubs.

Returning to Berlin as an actress, she appeared in more than 50 films, TV movies, and TV series playing roles of street girl, princcess, drug addict, stripper, secretary, thief, commissioner, Pakistani asylum seeker, German folk musician, Turkish cleaning woman, and loving psycho godmother.

Brauner launched a singing career, and dedicated herself to popularizing Yiddish classics that she knew from her childhood. She reinterpreted the songs, some of which are centuries old, in swing, jazz and pop, Balkan polka, Arab arabesques, South American rhythms, reggae, waltz, country, and tango elements. The songs captured the joy and the soul of the music.

The two videos below show the wide range of Brauner's Yiddish renditions. The first is a medley of *Love Story* and *My Way*, and the second is a lively version of *Di Grine Kuzine* (The Greenhorn

Cousin), a major hit in 1921 in the Yiddish music halls on Second Avenue in New York. Greenhorn was a common tag for newly arrived, un-Americanized, and unadapted immigrants.

Type the URLs into your browser address bar to see the videos:

https://youtu.be/5avn6kz77p4

https://youtu.be/gK8fqQaoREA

2000 Jewish Athletes Compete at Maccabi Games in Berlin

From July 27 to August 5, 2015, the 14th European Maccabi Games were held in Berlin.

Europe's biggest Jewish sports event took place in Germany for the first time in its history.

Where Jewish athletes were excluded from the Olympic Games in 1936, thousands sent a message for tolerance and openness and against anti-Semitism and racism this summer.

During the games, more than 2.000 Jewish sportswomen and sportsmen from more than 36 countries competed against each other in 19 disciplines in Berlin's Olympic Park.

As Yermi Brenner wrote in The Jewish Daily Forward,

The Games' opening ceremony took place in Berlin's Waldbühne – an amphitheatre built in the 1930's at the request of Nazi propaganda minister Joseph Goebbels. The ceremony's guest of honor was German president Joachim Gauck, who said he was very happy and moved by the fact that Berlin, which once discriminated against and humiliated Jewish athletes, is now hosting a Jewish sporting event.

Type the URLs into your browser address bar to see the videos:

https://youtu.be/mNYPcufPWPg

Part 2: UNEXPECTED TRACES IN JEWISH PLACES

Taiwanese Group Sings Hebrew Songs in Jerusalem

A group of Taiwanese thermal massage therapists visited Israel last year. But it's not just a group of Asian tourists visiting...there's a story behind it, and we think that with the Internet research we've done, we've only scratched the surface.

OK, here's what we found. In Taiwan there's a "Raphael Thermo Therapy Center" named in honor of Raphael Gamzou, former head of the Israel Economic and Cultural Office in Taipei—and de facto ambassador to Taiwan. The center is run by a healer known only as Master Lin -- and he has a loyal following of dozens of thermal therapy practitioners.

On the center's website, Ahavat Israel in Taiwan, Lin claims that his love for Israel and the Jewish people enables him to make an offer that many Jewish Israelis find hard to refuse -- and it's open only to Jewish residents of Israel.

With all expenses prepaid, Lin invites Israelis who are suffering from stress to fly to Taiwan and spend a few days in the specially equipped Raphael Thermo Therapy Center where they are given massages with a hand-held thermal device while the therapists sings Hebrew songs to them. The Center also provides a fully equipped apartment for each visitor to use while they spend time getting treatments in Taiwan.

Groups of therapists visit Israeli kibbutzim and towns. Last year they visited Jerusalem and made this video of their singing on the trip. The inclusion of a *Mashiach, Mashiach* song in the mix and letters on their website from Israelis who made the trip to Taiwan for treatment with promises that they will pray for the coming of the Messiah make us naturally suspicious of what's going on behind the scenes. But the absence of any overt prosyletizing leads us to give the group the benefit of the doubt and thank them for their generosity in bringing Jews in Israel relief from their physical and mental stresses while entertaining them with well-known Jewish and Israeli songs.

Type the URL into your browser address bar to see the video:

https://youtu.be/szY2ouysAdE

Japanese Klezmer Band Jinta-la-Mvta Performs at KulturfestNYC

One of the most unusual bands to perform at KulturfestNYC, the week-long festival of Jewish music was Jinta La-Mvta, a Japanese klezmer band. Yes, we said Japanese and klezmer in the same sentence.

The group was founded in 2004 by Ohkuma Wataru, clarinetist and bandleader of the groundbreaking Japanese experimental folk band Cicala Mvta and his partner and drummer Kogure Miwazo.

Considered as one of the few Klezmer experts in Japan, Wataru has also penned various pieces on Klezmer and Japanese liner notes of Klezmatics and Frank London.

We got a glimpse and sample of the band's music at the KulturfestNYC opening concert on June 14. The next day they performed at Joe's Pub at the Public.

We found a good sample of their Japanese klezmer style on YouTube and we're sharing it with you today.

Type the URL into your browser address bar to see the video:

https://youtu.be/a29EVNIGIyk

Hasidim Play and Sing "Samba Set"

Wedding music at Hasidic weddings is pretty predictable. That is, until now. At a recent wedding in Lakewood, New Jersey, the Meshorerim Choir sang and Naftuli Moshe Schnitzler played a "Samba Set" on the keyboard.

We found the music to be infectious as we swayed and looked for a dance partner to launch into a set of Latin American dances.

Do you think this will motivate Hasidic wedding guests to get out of their chairs and sweep across the dance floor? Will it lead to social dancing? Probably not, but who can predict what's next? The Rumba? Bossa Nova?

Type the URL into your browser address bar to see the video:

https://youtu.be/MDKXuKpNEyw

Haredi Musicians Play Beatles' Nowhere Man in Jerusalem

We've been running a series of occasional posts called *Jewish Traces in Unexpected Places*, where we share a slice of Jewish life in a location that you'd least expect to find it, such as bizarre versions of *Hava Nagila* and the Mud Men of Papua New Guinea reciting *Sh'ma Yisrael.*

Now it's time for a look at the reverse of this phenomenon that we'll call *Unexpected Traces in Jewish Places.* In this case the Jewish place is the Mamilla Shopping Mall in Jerusalem, and the unexpected trace is a couple of Haredi musicians playing guitar and singing one of the Beatles' most popular songs, *Nowhere Man.*

Not exactly what you'd expect a short distance from the Old City of Jerusalem, but thanks to Igor Trubin, who posted this and a few other selections that we'll be bringing you if you "like" this one, we can all enjoy this unexpected slice of Israeli life.

Type the URL into your browser address bar to see the video:

https://youtu.be/ndh4tRKTXhM

Hasidic Musicians Sing Pink Floyd in Jerusalem

About five weeks ago we shared a video of two Hasidic guitarists playing a Beatles song in a Jerusalem mall. We since learned their names, at least their first names. They're Gil and Arie, and one source says they're Breslover Hasidim. That's all we know about them.

They play in the Mamilla Mall, but mainly on Yafo Street along the route of the new light rail system. Whenever they play, they attract tourists, many of whom record their jam sessions on their cameras and smartphones. As a result, we're able to share some pretty good music, from unexpected sources.

Today's video shows them playing Wish You Were Here, a song by the 1960s psychedelic British group Pink Floyd.

We're usually surprised to find traces of Jewish life in far-flung places around the globe, which we call Jewish Traces in Unexpected Places. But we find it equally surprising to find very non-Jewish traces in musical performances by deeply religious Jews in Jerusalem, something we call Unexpected Traces in Jewish Places.

Type the URL into your browser address bar to see the video:

https://youtu.be/8LFaCov_63s

Gat Brothers Channel Eric Clapton in Jerusalem Mall

Ever since we discovered the YouTube posts by Igor Trubin of brothers Gil and Aryeh Gat singing in the streets of Jerusalem, we've been getting a lot of likes and requests for more.

In the last few months the brothers became sensations on the Israeli TV show "Rising Star" and achieved a second place finish in the competition. On the TV show they played songs by Simon and Garfunkel and The Eagles to an appreciative audience.

Among the street performances that Trubin captured was the brothers in Jerusalem's Mamilla Mall singing a renditon of Eric Clapton's hit *Tears From Heaven,* a song that he composed about the pain and loss Clapton felt following the death of his four-year-old son, Conor.

Type the URL into your browser address bar to see the video:

https://youtu.be/TxxSqPAB-Ho

Amazing Haredi Rabbis Sing Simon and Garfunkel on TV Show

Back in July we posted a video clip of two Haredi musicians playing the Beatles' *Nowhere Man* at the Mamilla Mall in Jerusalem. We discovered them while doing some late night surfing on YouTube to find a suitable post for the next day. But we didn't know anything about them, not even their names.

In August we found another clip of the same musicians playing the Pink Floyd song *Wish You Were Here* on Jaffa Road, and this time the comments revealed their first names -- Arie and Gil, and that they are Breslover Chasidim. But that's all. We thought they were very good, and so did you, from the reactions that we got to the blog posts. We wondered who they are, where they live, and when we would see more of them.

Well last week, they appeared on the new Israeli TV show "*Kochav haBa* (Rising Star) and when they played and sang Simon and Garfunkel's *Sounds of Silence*, the audience and the judges went wild. Thanks to the captions, we know they are brothers, Aryeh and Gil Gat. Aryeh, the older brother, is 48 and lives in Beit Shemesh. Gil, the younger brother, is 38, and lives in Jerusalem.

Type the URL into your browser address bar to see the video:

https://youtu.be/YwWFA04sqEo

A Yiddish Parody of "California Dreamin'"

When The Mamas and the Papas recorded *California Dreamin'* in 1966, we're sure they never expected that 48 years later a Yiddish parody of this classic pop song would appear.

But last week the Jewish People's Philharmonic Chorus posted their rendition of *Kalifornyer Kholem* on YouTube. The chorus is part of a modern Yiddish renaissance -- more than forty members strong, from students to retirees, a good number of whom speak or are learning Yiddish.

Their repertoire spans a century -- exciting oratorios and operettas, labor anthems, folksongs, and popular tunes -- all in Yiddish. Committed to strengthening Yiddish as a living language, they have commissioned and premiered new Yiddish choral works by half a dozen composers.

The JPPC shares the rich legacy of Yiddish song by performing year-round for old and young of all faiths at community centers, universities, K-12 schools, museums and places of worship throughout NYC's 4-state region. They have also performed at Carnegie Hall and Lincoln Center, at Ground Zero and the West Point Military Academy, as well as at the North American Jewish Choral Festival.

Type the URL into your browser address bar to see the video:
https://youtu.be/VDIf7booEAA

Rabbi and Gypsy Lady Play in the Streets of Jerusalem

When we came across a rabbi and a violinist playing in the rain on a Jerusalem street two weeks ago, we pulled out our smart phone and captured a few minutes of their antics to post here as a Jerusalem curiosity.

After some searching on the Internet, we discovered that the duo, known as The Rabbi and Gypsy Lady, are regular performers in Kikar Zion (Zion Square) and also on stage in clubs and theaters around Israel.

Who are these street and theater performers? Rabbi Tomer Peretz's day job is as a teacher of Torah and Talmud, but he is also a singer, composer and guitarist, and can be found often at the junction of Ben Yehuda Street and Jaffa Road in Zion Square. His musical partner is Alexandra Kanarit. This "Gypsy Lady" is a violinist and composer from the Ukraine.

Together they are The Rabbi & Gypsy Lady who for most of their lives have created music and shared their love with other people through art performance. They love what they do and they do what they love.

For the last three years both of them have separately been engaged in street shows, making people happy. One day they met each other at Kikar Zion, Jerusalem, immediately connected with mutual common energy. Two people who became one through art and now The Rabbi and Gypsy Lady perform together.

They play a wide range of Israeli songs and their original

compositions, but they seem especially drawn to rock music. Two of their favorites are *Stairway to Heaven*, the Led Zeppelin standby, and *Ain't no Sunshine*, the song made popular by Bill Withers.

Here is one of their performances of *Ain't no Sunshine* at the Theatron HaStudio in Haifa.

Type the URL into your browser address bar to see the video:

https://youtu.be/p3-UG3nlZLg

A Country and Western Shalom Aleichem

Beit T'shuvah is a Los Angeles based community with a mission to guide individuals and families towards a path of living well, so that wrestling souls can recover from addiction and learn how to properly heal.

The Beit T'Shuvah faith-based model, founded on authenticity and wholeness, integrates spirituality, psychotherapy, Jewish teachings, the 12 Steps, and the creative arts. They are a compassionate, supportive community, devoted to building an empowering sense of belonging and purpose to everyone who seeks it.

They also have a band, and last week they recorded a unique Outlaw Country Shabbat service with all the familiar songs in the Friday night liturgy sung to classic Country and Western tunes.

So put on your boots and cowboy hats, and join them in welcoming Shabbat with *Shalom Aleichem* sung to the tune of Lookin' Out My Back Door as sung by Creedence Clearwater Revival.

Street Shofar Man Takes His Shtick to Israel

OK, you can argue that Israel is not an unexpected place to hear the shofar, unlike the streets of Los Angeles and New York, where Street Shofar Man blew his horn before Rosh Hashanah last year.

At the Western Wall, OK. But in a Bedouin camp? In a Tel Aviv night club?

Last September we posted two visits of Michael Braus, who calls himself Street Shofar Man, to the streets of Los Angeles and New York as a wake up call to what's possible for ourselves and our world at the start of the Jewish new year.

Now Street Shofar treks across Israel -- from Jerusalem's Old City to military bases, from Bedouin villages to posh suburban parks and hot Tel Aviv night clubs -- bringing the shofar's eternal message of peace, understanding, and new possibilty. Isn't it the time of year for us to ask ourselves what we stand for?

The videos were produced by IKAR, a progressive, egalitarian Jewish community in Los Angeles.

Type the URL into your browser address bar to see the video:

https://youtu.be/awATvJ9LK9o

Amish and Mennonite Group Visits the Western Wall

A delegation of Amish/Mennonite communities visited Israel in November 2012 to express their commitment to Israel and the Jewish People.

The Jerusalem Post reported:
Although there is no shortage of extraordinary sights at the Wall, the visit by a group of 31 Amish people (29 Americans and 2 Canadians) had people staring in wonder as the group filled the air with their heartfelt hymns. The group came to Israel to apologize to the Jewish people for not previously recognizing the Jews as the chosen people and for not doing more to prevent persecution of the Jews in the past.

The group expressed the purpose of their visit: "We would like to meet and bless the people of Israel, to show our support, especially in the area of repentance, and acknowledgment of our errors, such as having rejected them as God's chosen people."

"We would like to meet with city officials and other leaders who would give us a few minutes of their time. We, the Amish and Anabaptist people turned away from Jewish nation, while they were in their darkest hour of need. We hardened our hearts against them, we left them - never lifting our voices in protest against the atrocities that were committed against them. We want to publicly repent of this and acknowledge our support of Israel."

This video shows the group united in song at the Western Wall. Type the URL into your browser address bar to see the video:

https://youtu.be/6iT7SpxDOoM

Pope Francis Confers Catholic Knighthood on Orthodox Rabbi

Rabbi Arthur Schneier, whose Park East Synagogue in Manhattan was the site of a visit by Pope Benedict XVI in 2008, was named a papal knight of St. Sylvester, the oldest Catholic order of knighthood on Monday.

The 85-year-old Orthodox rabbi, a Holocaust survivor, has led his synagogue since 1962.

As James Barron reported the The New York Times,

Rabbi Schneier has been a presence at conferences in world trouble spots to promote tolerance and resolve ethnic and religious conflicts. He founded the interfaith Appeal of Conscience Foundation in 1965.

"You know this award to our beloved Rabbi Schneier comes from Pope Francis," Cardinal Dolan said before pinning a Knight's Cross on the rabbi. "It's Pope Francis's very touching, very tender way of confirming him in the good works that he's done on behalf of religious freedom, international peace and justice."

A crowd of dignitaries looked on. Among them were former Secretary of State Henry A. Kissinger; former Mayor David N. Dinkins; United States Representative Carolyn B. Maloney, a Democrat of New York; and Raymond W. Kelly, the former police commissioner.

Several religious leaders and officials also attended the ceremony, including Archbishop Demetrios, the spiritual leader of Greek Orthodox Christians of America; Archbishop Khajag Barsamian of the Armenian Church of America; Imam Al-Hajj Talib Abdur-Rashid of the Mosque of Islamic Brotherhood; Rabbi Joseph Potasnik, the executive vice president of the New York Board of Rabbis; Abraham H. Foxman, the national director of the Anti-Defamation League; and Rabbi Michael Miller, the executive vice president and chief executive of the Jewish Community Relations Council of New York. Rabbi Schneier's son, Rabbi Marc Schneier, also attended.

Type the URL into your browser address bar to see the video:

https://youtu.be/wzn7dZbRR04

Part 3: HAVA NAGILA AROUND THE WORLD

Hava Nagila's appeal somehow crosses geographic, cultural, and religious boundaries to keep it popular all over the world. So we collected some of the most unusual performances of this song which some love and others think is the most overplayed Jewish song ever. We think you'll really enjoy watching and listening as we travel across all continents to see this classic Jewish song performed in some very unexpected ways and in some very unexpected places.

Hava Nagila, Texas Style

Christians United for Israel (CUFI) has held 95 Nights to Honor Israel in cities all across America since February 2006. The evenings attract thousands of Christians who rally to support Israel and contribute millions of dollars every year to Israeli charities.

Israeli music and dancing are a big part of these evenings, and in October 2008 one of the biggest rallies was held in San Antonio, Texas, home of Pastor John Hagee's Cornerstone Church.

The Cornerstone Orchestra and Choir performed a very energetic Texas style version of Hava Nagila and medleys of popular Israeli songs. Here is a Hava Nagila that's unlike any you've heard. Wanna get pumped up and start your day on a bright and sunny note? Just click below and enjoy!

Type the URL into your browser address bar to see the video:

http://youtu.be/2WF6irnzAiI

Thailand Burlesque Adopts Hava Nagila

From Thailand comes a burlesque version of Hava Nagila. The singer starts out with a few bars of the title song from the film *Exodus*, and then launches into Hava Nagila. So sit back, watch, enjoy, and have some laughs. It's OK to laugh out loud (LOL). We did!

Type the URL into your browser address bar to see the video:

http://youtu.be/buysVLsTDrs

Hava Nagila Scores Big in Thailand

In April 2010, around the time we started our series of *Hava Nagila* around the world, we found and posted a somewhat risque version of the popular song -- actually a burlesque version. We regarded it as an oddity. What a surprise this week to find a more mainstream performance on Thailand's popular TV show, *The Voice Thailand*.

The Voice is a reality talent show focusing on singing competition. It's a worldwide series that started in the Netherlands as *The Voice of Holland* in 2010. Soon after, many other countries including the USA have adapted the format and are airing their national versions. It's part of a talent competition phenomenon that includes *American Idol, Britain's Got Talent* and Israel's *Kochav Nolad* (A Star is Born).

We don't know how far this singer will get in the talent competition and how many times *Hava Nagila* will resound through the airwaves in Thailand, but for the time being, we can just enjoy the performance.

Type the URL into your browser address bar to see the video:

https://youtu.be/7BRiCvqalJk

It's Hava Nagila Again, with the King of Russian Pop Music

Now join us as we journey to Russia to listen to Philip Kirkorov, celebrated Bulgarian singer and king of Russian pop, bring his energy to this Jewish classic in a staging that has a troupe of singers, dancers, musicians and (well, see for yourself.)

Type the URL into your browser address bar to see the video:

https://youtu.be/lU-2NoZ9hpY

Hava Nagila (or is it Ave Maria?) by Hahamishia Hakamerit

Here's yet another version of Hava Nagila, this one by the satirical Israeli group Hahamishia Hakamerit, which they performed in a weekly sketch comedy TV show that ran from 1993 to 1997. Funny, that melody's familiar, but it sure doesn't sound like the traditional Hava Nagila.

Type the URL into your browser address bar to see the video:

http://youtu.be/ZWNb8cCBsGU

Another Hava Nagila, This One for British Teenyboppers

A couple of years ago British pop singer Lauren Rose recorded an English version of Hava Nagila as a Chanukah present for her grandfather. Little did she expect that the sexy, slightly racy version would electrify her teeny-bopper fan base and become the Number One *Christmas* song of 2007.

As Jordan Namerow wrote in Jewish Women's Archive's Jewesses with Attitude blog,

Who knew that "Hava Nagila" could be "sexy" ... or "racy"...? Lauren Rose (formerly Lauren Goldberg), a Jewess from the UK, has given this familiar (and perhaps tiresome) traditional Hebrew folk song a somewhat dirty, teeny-bopper twist.

Her new top-of-the-charts hit "Hava Nagila (Baby Let's Dance)" -- the anticipated No. 1 Christmas song in the UK... huh? -- is creating a stir in the blogosphere and on YouTube, sparking many reactions, from pride and awe-struck praise, to disgust and outrage. Performed in a ruffley mini-skirt and seductive, pouty expressions, Rose's lyrics fuse the original Hebrew words of "Hava Nagila" with: *"Hold me, hold me... move our bodies, baby let's dance"* and *"it's ok to let go, it's ok if you wanna show... lose it... just jump, just jump... close your eyes and breathe."*

Type the URL into your browser address bar to see the video:

http://youtu.be/PgdWwfCZxGE

Violina Plays Electric HavaNagila in Estonia

What's the most likely song to be played by three talented Estonian electric violinists in ultra-tight dresses? Isn't the answer obvious? Of course. It's Hava Nagila.

These musicians with their distinctive white violins, performed on the Estonian TV show, *Tahed Muusikas*, or Music Stars. They play a wide range of pop music and Eastern European folk music.

Type the URL into your browser address bar to see the video:

http://youtu.be/poOCAxKOHtM

Hava Nagila Resonates in Southern Poland

In Southeastern Poland, close to the borders with and Slovakia, the sounds of *Hava Nagila* were heard in the streets of Rzesziw in 2010. The song was featured in a concert outdoors in the rain, with a large chorus and orchestra leading the way, and the large crowd, holding umbrellas, joining in the singing.

As we point out in the headline above, this is a Jewish trace, but not a Jewish group singing. It's a Christian choir started by two Catholic priests in the area of Rzeszow, with much the same energy as the Cornerstone Singers from Texas expended in their country version of Hava Nagila, which we reported on way back in November 2009, our first blog post about the spread of this song around the world.

Type the URL into your browser address bar to see the video:

https://youtu.be/cWPPedsKMUc

An Indian Bollywood Production of Hava Nagila

There must be something in the music of Hava Nagila that appeals to people around the world in so many cultures. It has to be the music and not the lyrics, because if you listen carefully you'll find that most singers mispronounce the words and don't seem to have a clue as to their meaning.

Here is a lively dancing version in a Bollywood movie made in India.

Type the URL into your browser address bar to see the video:

http://youtu.be/FdG9P1MsU5A

Even in Iran, They Play Hava Nagila

A popular musical instrument in Iran is the santur, best translated as a hammered dulcimer. In this video, an Iranian street musician plays an instrumental version of Hava Nagila on the santur. The song itself starts about a minute and a half into the video.

Type the URL into your browser address bar to see the video:

http://youtu.be/tVhxQxZRbww

Who's Singing Hava Nagila? Is It Really The Beatles?

This version of Hava Nagila takes us back to the 1960s, when Beatlemania was raging in the music world. But did the Beatles really sing *Hava Nagila*? You'll do a double take, as we did, watching the video below. It's remarkable how much the singers look like the Fab Four, especially Paul and Ringo.

But it's really a performance by a Beatles tribute band, The Moptops, taken from a real movie parody of *A Hard Day's Night*, called *A Hard Day's Day*. The nine-minute film, directed by David Kessler, depicts a day in the life of the band. *Hava Nagila* is the song played in the movie's climax, set at a Bar Mitzvah celebration.

Type the URL into your browser address bar to see the video:

http://youtu.be/AOxVXQlZXqI

Santa Claus Plays Hava Nagila on the Violin

If you happened to be in Honolulu, Hawaii in December 2011 and thought you heard a familiar tune coming out of Santa Claus' violin, you were right.

We don't know his name or what prompted this street Santa to play *Hava Nagila* on his violin on a hot December day in Hawaii, but it's just another example of how *Hava Nagila* has become popular not just with Jews, but in almost every location on the planet.

Type the URL into your browser address bar to see the video:

http://youtu.be/_S6C5nyVkSw

Hava Nagila is a Show Stopper in Paraguay

Just when we thought we were running out of countries that give their unique styling to *Hava Nagila*, along comes a new one -- Paraguay.

We don't know what motivated the quartet of Paraguayan musicians that calls themselves *Los Paranas del Paraguay* to end their concert at a club in San Antonio, Texas with a rousing performance of *Hava Nagila*, but that's exactly what they did.

We've seen this phenomenon all over the world and we've shared many of the videos with you. And still they keep coming. There's just something about *Hava Nagila* that gets to every nationality and every culture. Its global popularity would probably have been a big surprise to Abraham Zvi Idelsohn, who composed the song based on a Ukrainian folk dance in 1918 to celebrate the British victory in Palestine during World War I as well as the Balfour Declaration.

Type the URL into your browser address bar to see the video:

http://youtu.be/ZyfX-8OwcGo

Hava Nagila Is Choice of German Ice Skating Team

When the 16 ice skaters who comprise the synchronized ice skating Dream Team from Germany's Lower Saxony province stepped onto the ice in a competition in 2009, what song do you think they chose to skate and dance to? If you've been reading this blog for a while, you've probably guessed it already. Of course, it's *Hava Nagila*, the song that has been performed all over the world in the most unusual places.

And we thought we'd have to wait for *Moshiach* to come before seeing something like this.

So enjoy the six minute skating routine, which starts with *Shema Yisrael* before moving into *Hava Nagila*. If you look carefully at the dozen or so flags at one end of the arena (at around 5 minutes into the performance) you'll see the Israeli flag among them.

Type the URL into your browser address bar to see the video:

http://youtu.be/yPmdocLoIA4

In British Columbia, Hava Nagila and Belly Dancing Go Together

We've brought you renditions of Hava Nagila in more countries and provinces than we can name, but until now we haven't found one from British Columbia. This Canadian province, north of Seattle, Washington, is home to two musical genres that we wouldn't have put together, but they seem to have found each other.

The first is guitar, as exemplified by Colin Godbout, the Global Guitarist of Vancouver, and the second is the art of belly dancing, as performed by Asmira, who has been running a school of oriental belly dance for the past 24 years in Victoria, also in British Columbia.

Last month, Godbout joined Asmira in Victoria for a concert of music from countries along the route of the Orient Express, which ran between Paris and Istanbul. At the end of this performance, they joined in an encore of Hava Nagila, ending with a flourish of Miserlou, a popular Greek song about an Egyptian girl, usually played as a dance at Jewish weddings. Go figure, and enjoy!

Click on URL to see the video:

http://youtu.be/q9vVNPm6Hqo

Hava Nagila in the Streets of Italy

If you happened to be walking in the Piazza Vecchia of Bergamo, Italy in May 2011, you may have run into BARABONZIBONZIBO, a four part busking team of street musicians whose aim is to get real reactions from everyday people.

Wherever they perform, the group tries to turn a street into a party venue, to wake people's senses up, trying to break down the wall of indifference. They also have open instrument cases prominently displayed for pleased customers to reward them with some extra cash.

So what song did they pick to upload to YouTube as an example of their work? Hava Nagila, of course.

Type the URL into your browser address bar to see the video:

http://youtu.be/F-plPu9Hl-M

Hava Nagila in the Shetland Islands Near the Arctic Circle

Regular readers of the Jewish Humor Central blog know that we have been following the trail of *Hava Nagila* around the world and visiting far-flung locations where singing and dancing to this classic Jewish melody defy any logic.

This journey has certainly led us to see unusual places and to learn about world geography, but this may be the most remote location and most bizarre rendition of the classic song yet.

First, the geography lesson. Over 300 miles north of Edinburgh lie the Shetland Islands, more than half-way between London and the Arctic Circle. The Shetland Islands are as far North as Helsinki (Finland), Hudson Bay (Canada), Alaska (USA) and Leningrad (Russia). However, the climate in Shetland is not as extreme as in any of these other places, thanks to the moderating effect of the very northern end of the Gulf Stream.

The islands themselves belong to Scotland, and are part of the UK, so UK traffic regulations apply, Scottish Law applies, Shetland is part of the UK Postal network, and everyone speaks standard English (although the old Shetland dialect is still heard occasionally).

Each year the Shetland islanders celebrate the abiding influence of the Vikings, who arrived in Shetland just over 1000 years ago, with the largest fire festival in Europe, called Up Helly Aa.

After a torch-light procession of up to a thousand "guizers" through the streets of Lerwick a full-size replica Viking longship is ceremonially burned. The "guizers" and onlookers then repair to local halls for a night of revelry, dancing and partying. (Guizers are mummers or actors in a folk play, usually wearing outlandish costumes.)

After the burning of the ship, the party continues, as 48 squads, consisting of exactly 902 guizers, all disguised with a particular theme in mind, visit eleven halls in rotation.

At every hall each squad performs its 'act', perhaps a skit on local events, a dance display in spectacular costume, or a topical send-up of a popular TV show or pop group. Every guizer has a duty (as the *Up Helly A* Song says) to dance with at least one of the ladies in the hall, before taking yet another dram.

Would you believe that on March 11, 2011 at the South Mainland Up Helly Aa one of the squads dressed up as participants in a Chassidic wedding and after the ceremony (with one of the authentic *Sheva B'rachot*) sang and danced a rousing version of *Hava Nagila?* You have to see it to believe it, so here's the video.

Type the URL into your browser address bar to see the video:

http://youtu.be/lXo4pl9jW4o

Indian Band Amrutam Gamaya Performs Hava Nagila

If you think you've heard the most beautiful rendition of Hava Nagila, then guess again. Recently the Israeli folk song was performed on, of all places, the popular Indian talent show Music Mojo by a band by the name of Amrutam Gamaya.

While the tune is normally fast paced and uplifting, this version definitely stands apart from other versions of the song. Although the tune does quicken near its end, the song is less upbeat and Amrutha Suresh, the lead singer of the group, has a hauntingly beautiful voice.

Type the URL into your browser address bar to see the video:

https://youtu.be/h7lGRirxV5g

Jewish Sword Dancer Wins with Hava Nagila in Korea

Did you know that Aly Raisman is not the only Jewish American to win a world championship by performing to the music of Hava Nagila? Of course, we all know about Raisman's achievement in gymnastics, winning the gold medal at the London Summer Olympics for her floor exercise.

Meanwhile, 5,500 miles away in Daejeon City, South Korea, practitioners of the ancient Korean martial art of Haedong Gumdo have been competing for medals in an international competition.

The bronze medal was won by Josh Segal, performing the sword dance to a medley of Israeli songs, including Nigun Atik, Hava Nagila, and Erev Shel Shoshanim.

Type the URL into your browser address bar to see the video:

http://youtu.be/VoF_CUCeZuU

Hava Nagila is Alive and Well in Buenos Aires Flash Mob

The Abasto de Buenos Aires was the central wholesale fruit and vegetable market in Buenos Aires, Argentina, from 1893 to 1984. Since 1999, it has served as a shopping mall.

In June 2012, shoppers in the Abasto Mall were treated to a spontaneous outpouring of Jewish song and dance to the music of Hava Nagila by a flash mob brought in by YOK, a project of the American Jewish Joint Distribution Committee. The dance was in celebration of Dia de la Bandera, an annual holiday to celebrate the Argentinian national flag. Because it was performed in Argentina, the dancers couldn't resist incorporating elements of the tango, and while they were at it, also included a few measures of *To Life, L'Chayim!*

Today a vibrant Jewish population is integrated into the towns and business of Buenos Aires. There are city fairs for Jewish holidays, hosted by YOK Time, a non-profit organization that encourages approaching Judaism “in your own way”. YOK’s Rosh Hashana fair offers attendees free apples and honey to celebrate the New Year and goods from local Jewish artists, and on Passover you can participate in a gefilte fish contest and listen to Klezmer music, all in the barrio of Palermo.

YOK, which stands for *‘Yo OK’* or ‘I am OK,’ creates these urban festivals to “establish a space where people can gather to share their Jewish culture and traditions with the whole community,” according to Dana Jones of Project YOK.

Type the URL into your browser address bar to see the video:

http://youtu.be/Dv61TIkKPt4

Thailand Ladyboys Sing Hava Nagila

Today's blog post combines two of our recurring themes -- Unusual juxtapositions of Jewish music and culture in strange environments and the continuing popularity of Hava Nagila around the globe.

We wouldn't expect to encounter a group of transgendered singers and dancers performing a rousing version of Hava Nagila on a stage in Bangkok, Thailand, but that's exactly what we found. This is the 48th version of Hava Nagila that we've posted since we started Jewish Humor Central five years ago.

Bangkok's entertainers include a large number of what they call Ladyboys, and why these performers chose to exhibit their talents to one of the most popular Jewish melodies is beyond us.

If you think the whole thing is somehow backwards, take a look at the writing on the stage wall. It's Hava Nagila in English, Thai, Chinese, Japanese, and Hebrew, but the Hebrew letters are backwards, written from left to right instead of from right to left.

Type the URL into your browser address bar to see the video:

https://youtu.be/MZQF7PvePSM

German Children's Choir Sings Hava Nagila

Hava Nagila and *Hevenu Shalom Aleichem* have become popular worldwide, and we have posted some renditions of these songs being performed in places that you would least expect to hear them.

Here is another example of how Jewish music can pop up unexpectedly, in this case in a church in the small town of Osterode, in Lower Saxony, Germany. And you don't have to be Jewish to sing it.

The Rainbow Children, a children's choir from Osterode, led by Rita J. Sührig sing along with the Black Ravens from Förste led by Holger Schlenczek and the soloist Siegfried Seyfarth in the Market Church in Osterode front of an enthusiastic audience, the Israeli songs Hava Nagila and Hevenu Shalom Aleichem.

Type the URL into your browser address bar to see the video:

http://youtu.be/CMFmVaXUeQU

A Hava Nagila Encore from Korea

The Busan Harmony Choir (www.bsharmony.com) is an amateur choir in Busan, South Korea that includes teachers, doctors, professors, businessmen, salarymen, housekeepers, and students. They performed in concert on June 25, 2011.

After we posted a video of the choir singing Hevenu Shalom Aleichem (see below), we received a nice note from Y. S. Chang, chief of the choir. He wrote that Korean history shares some similarity with Jewish history.

"A lot of countries invaded Korea continuously for more than 1,000 years. Many Korean (Chosun Dynasty) young men and women were dragged to China (Qing Dynasty) 450 years ago after the war with Qing (China). Also, Japan invaded Korea many times. Finally, the Korean War broke out in 1950 and separated South and North Korea. Because of the Korean War, a lot of people died and their families were broken up."

"Now, Koreans know the value of 'Peace' as much as Jews. So, I think both peoples have a common understanding of 'Peace'. When we sing 'Hevenu Shalom Aleichem', we feel the Jewish wish for peace."

"Anyway, it is a good opportunity for me to understand more about Jews, and thanks for your posting our concert."

We're following up by including a video of the Busan Harmony Choir in a concert performance of *Hava Nagila.*

Type the URL into your browser address bar to see the video:

http://youtu.be/BbNEVTA1Irw

Charles Aznavour and Enrico Macias Sing Hava Nagila

Charles Aznavour and Enrico Macias have been singing in concerts worldwide since the 1960s. Aznavour, who has been called the French Frank Sinatra, was born in Paris to Armenian immigrants in 1924. And he's still singing. In 1998, he was named Entertainer of the Century by CNN. He was recognized as the century's outstanding performer, with nearly 18% of the total vote, edging out Elvis Presley and Bob Dylan. He has sung for presidents, popes, and royalty.

Macias, a native of French Algeria, has also performed around the world, primarily in Europe and the Middle East. Born to Jewish parents in 1938, he has not been allowed to return to Algeria because of his ongoing support for Israel.

In 1973, Aznavour and Macias performed a rousing version of Hava Nagila at a concert that was recently posted to YouTube. Aznavour, who is not Jewish, and Macias, who is, take turns tweaking the song to bring out some elements that sound almost cantorial.

Type the URL into your browser address bar to see the video:

http://youtu.be/QTRS30B4b6s

A Russian Folk Instrument Version of Hava Nagila

A very Russian folk ensemble with the English name *Style-Quartet* and a forceful, almost cantorial, singer named Maya Balashova, recently filled a concert hall in Russia where they performed a rousing version of Hava Nagila.

In this version, Balashova is accompanied by musicians playing the balalaika, a huge triangular guitar-like instrument, the domra, a mandolin-like instrument, and the bayan, a Russian accordion.

Type the URL into your browser address bar to see the video:

http://youtu.be/88wm9KGvu9w

Hava Nagila Gets Indian Bhangra Treatment in Vancouver

What do the Israeli Hora and Indian Bhangra have in common? Apparently, something, because in May 2011 there was a performance in Vancouver of a fusion of Israeli Hora and Indian Bhangra by the Jewish Community Centre of Greater Vancouver and Surrey India Arts Club.

The two groups performed together at the Vancouver Art Gallery Georgia Plaza, Vancouver, BC, Canada.

The performance begins with what appears to be a traditional hora with the music of Hava Nagila. After two minutes, the Israeli dancers exchange places with a troupe of Indian dancers who complete the hora and transition to a folk dance set to Bhangra music.

Bhangra is a form of Indian dance and music originated by farmers in the Punjabi region in the 11th century to celebrate the coming of the harvest season. The specific moves of bhangra reflect the manner in which villagers farmed their land. The performances are colorful and lively and we hope you enjoy them.

Type the URL into your browser address bar to see the video:

http://youtu.be/cR1kloYoPjs

Aly Raisman Wins Gymnastics Gold to Hava Nagila

Olympic Gold Medal winning gymnast Alexandra (Aly) Raisman was a double source of nachas for the Jewish community worldwide in August 2012 when she became the first American to win the gold medal for the floor exercise in gymnastics.

After receiving the medal, she said that it was a special victory because it came on the 40th anniversary of the massacre of 11 Israeli athletes at the Munich Olympic Games in 1972.

As Agence France-Presse reported:

Alexandra Raisman said winning a gold medal on the 40th anniversary of the Munich massacre made her achievement "special" after she triumphed in the Olympic women's gymnastics floor final on Tuesday.

Raisman, who is Jewish, performed her floor routine to the backing of Hebrew folk song 'Hava Nagila' and earned a score of 15.600 points to claim her third medal of the London Games at North Greenwich Arena.

The 18-year-old American said that she had not selected the music specifically to coincide with the anniversary, but added that she was proud to have marked the occasion.

"Having that floor music wasn't intentional, but the fact it was on the 40th anniversary is special and winning the gold today means a lot to me," she said.

"If there had been a moment's silence, I would have supported it and respected it."

Type the URL into your browser address bar to see the video of Raisman's winning performance:

http://youtu.be/Z8gLzAfZMFA

"Hava Nagila the Movie" Puts It All Together

Producer and director Roberta Grossman worked for more than two years to capture the essence of the song *Hava Nagila*, arguably the most covered song in the Jewish music repertory. She met with potential donors, encouraging them to contribute to the cause of creating the documentary, called *Hava Nagila -- What is it?*

The film is a documentary romp through the history, mystery, and meaning of the great Jewish standard. Funny, deep and unexpected, the film celebrates 100 years of Jewish history, culture and spirituality. It reveals the power of music to bridge cultural divides and bring us together as human beings.

In October 2012, The New York Times carried a story about the film and the related exhibition in the Museum of Jewish Heritage, in Lower Manhattan.

Here is the 10 minute preview that was used for fund raising. Looks like it was successful. The 73 minute movie was shown in film festivals in 2012 and is scheduled to open for theatrical release in New York in March 2013.

Click on the URL to see the preview:

http://youtu.be/Qz34klOPUis

Balkan Bistro Street Band Plays Hava Nagila

In the four years that we've been posting videos, we included 39 versions of *Hava Nagila*, as performed all over the world, many in very unlikely places. Athough it's been awhile since the most recent post, we haven't stopped looking for new and ususual renditions.

Today we're posting our fortieth *Hava Nagila*, as played by the *Balkan Bistro Street Band*. The band is a project involving six young musicians and fans of Balkan music in general in Eastern Europe. With suitable training for playing in place and on the march, they try to raise awareness and infect their listeners with their passion for Balkan music and its sounds and rhythms.

They seem to play mainly in cities in Italy, marching through the streets in loose formation while they play. In this non-marching version of *Hava Nagila*, they start the melody about 30 seconds into the video, play the song for two minutes, launch into some improv for two minutes, and then return to Hava Nagila.

Type the URL into your browser address bar to see the video:

https://youtu.be/LQmhLNvp8oo

Indonesian Muslim Choir Sings Hava Nagila

Islam is the dominant religion in Indonesia, which also has a larger Muslim population than any other country in the world, with approximately 202.9 million identified as Muslim (88.2% of Indonesia's total population of 237 million). So what are the odds that the Indonesian Student Choir at Padjadjaran University would post a video on YouTube of them singing a rousing version of Hava Nagila?

Not very high, you'd say? Well, take a look at this video of the students adding their voices to the many around the world who have sung Hava Nagila (love it or hate it, you can't deny that it's the most recognized Jewish song). We've already posted more than 30 versions and we don't expect to run out of them any time soon.

Type the URL into your browser address bar to see the video:

https://youtu.be/n7wz6qvu_No

David Garrett and Martynas Play Hava Nagila in Berlin

David Garrett, a record-breaking German pop and crossover violinist and recording artist, and Martynas Levickis, a young Lithuanian accordion virtuoso, got together at a concert in Berlin and electrified the crowd with a rousing rendition of Hava Nagila.

Garrett attended the Keshet Eilon Masterclasses in Israel in the summers of 1997, 1998, 1999 and 2002. Keshet Eilon is a music center established in the year 1990, located in Kibbutz Eilon, Israel. Its mission is to be a source of strength and support for young gifted violinists.

Martynas recently completed his degree at the Royal Academy of Music in London, and has acquired all the knowledge and technical expertise of a professional classical musician, but he sees classical music as just one part of his personal mix.

Type the URL into your browser address bar to see the video:

https://youtu.be/dADsgbNIuug

In Cuba, It's Not Hava Nagila, But Havana Guila

Continuing our review of Hava Nagila performances around the world, we came across the singer called Candela singing the world's most popular Jewish song, with a Latin accent. It's part of an album called Tel Aviv-Habana.

The CD is filled with familiar Jewish and Israeli songs, all set to a lively Cuban Latin beat. You can listen to generous samples of all the songs on the album on the Israel Music website. In addition to Havana Guila, it includes Hallelujah, Al Kol Eleh, Adon Olam, Bashana Haba'ah, Barkhenu, Hevenu Shalom Aleichem, Yerushalayim Shel Zahav, and Tel Aviv-Habana.

So put on your dancing shoes, sing, dance, and enjoy!

Type the URL into your browser address bar to see the video:

http://youtu.be/xHlRAeZkBhg

A Rousing Medley of Songs by Texas Church Choir

Back in November 2009, when Jewish Humor Central was just getting started and we had just a handful of subscribers, we posted a spirited version of *Hava Nagila* performed by the Cornerstone Orchestra and Choir.

The musicians are members of Christians United for Israel (CUFI), based in San Antonio, Texas, home of Pastor John Hagee's Cornerstone Church

CUFI has held Nights to Honor Israel in cities all across America since February 2006. The evenings attract thousands of Christians who rally to support Israel and contribute millions of dollars every year to Israeli charities.

Today we found the complete medley of Hebrew songs that ended with the rendition of *Hava Nagila*. Here is a medley that's unlike any you've heard. Besides Hava Nagila, it includes *Mayim Mayim, Eleh Chomdo Libi, David Melech Yisrael, Nigun Atik,* and *Hevenu Shalom Aleichem.*

Type the URL into your browser address bar to see the video:

https://youtu.be/dMR-j4xpA9I

Ray Charles and David Ben Gurion Sing Hava Nagila

In 1973 Ray Charles performed a concert in Tel Aviv. The concert film "Ray Charles: Soul of the Holy Land August 1973" documents the legendary performer's historic Tel Aviv concert and includes footage of him visiting some of the most renowned religious sites in the world.

The 17-song set list includes many beloved hits including a cover of the Beatles' "The Long and Winding Road," "Let the Good Times Roll," "I Can't Stop Loving You," and "Yesterday."

During the concert, Charles met with David Ben Gurion, and the two sang Hava Nagila together. Here's a rare look at two very successful people in two very different fields coming together to celebrate Israel through one of its most popular songs.

Type the URL into your browser address bar to see the video:

https://youtu.be/HZUjvjP3fVc

Streets of Paris Resound to Hava Nagila with Gad Elbaz

In light of the recent terror attacks on French journalists and Jews, and in a show of solidarity for the Jewish community of France, Israeli superstar Gad Elbaz has released a new music video to a contemporary upbeat version of Hava Nagila.

Hava Nagila which means "Lets be happy" is the most well-known Jewish song, and serves as a universal call to unite all people in song. Gad Elbaz along with Jews, Muslim and Christians dancers, dance at the Place De La Republic, Shanzelize and the streets of Paris accompanied by an eastern European Klezmer Band.

"Despite the French army presence at every Jewish site, we still felt the fear and heightened tensions everywhere. That however, did not hold us back from singing and dancing to Hava Nagila in the streets of Paris, and spreading the joy." said producer-Director Daniel Finkelman." Its all about people taking a stand and refusing to be bullied, we will not hide our identity as Jews, we are proud to be Jewish" Added Gad Elbaz.

Elbaz already achieved international success by the age of 26 with three number one hit songs, *Halayla Zeh Hazman*, *Or* and *Al Neharot Bavel.* All of his CD's have climbed high on the charts and sold over 100,000 copies in Israel alone. Gad began to sing and write music at age four. He first appeared with his father Benny Elbaz, a popular Israeli singer, accompanying him on the hit song *Father I Love You.*

Gad's music intentionally captures both the observant and secular listener by mixing original and biblical texts with ballads, harmonies, middle-eastern rhythms and modern pop. Many of the songs are a collaboration between him and his wife Moran, where he composes the music and she writes the lyrics.

Type the URL into your browser address bar to see the video:

https://youtu.be/BGrzh3W-F-c

Gypsy Philharmonic Orchestra in Budapest Plays Hava Nagila

You'd think that with the 48 versions of *Hava Nagila* that we've posted here, we would be satisfied and stop looking for more.

But then we surfed some more and found a version by the Gypsy Philharmonic Orchestra, which mixes the traditional gypsy violin and the airs of the Hungarian and Yiddish repertoire with the great classical composers works such as Johannes Brahms, Jacques Offenbach, Pablo de Sarasate, Johann Strauss Father & Son, Pyotr Illyich Tchaikovsky and contemporary composers such as John Williams.

So we just had to share it with you, and here it is, as recorded last December in Budapest, Hungary.

Type the URL into your browser address bar to see the video:

https://youtu.be/Oo41ujvaIDs

Japanese Ukuleles Play Hava Nagila in Tokyo Shrine

How likely is it to see and hear a group of Japanese ukulele players perform Hava Nagila on stage at a Shinto shrine on a mountaintop in Tokyo? Not very likely, but we found a video of just such a happening.

The players are a group called Ukulele Afternoon. They have been performing ukulele concerts in Japan for more than 20 years.

Ukulele Afternoon embodies everything about Japanese culture - they embrace traditional and modern approaches to music and art. Their music has all the excitement of a punk rock band combined with the sensitivity of a chamber orchestra.

The first three minutes of the video shows the ensemble playing Hava Nagila, and then they play other songs.

Type the URL into your browser address bar to see the video:

https://youtu.be/-tGWAgqKFxQ

Sunday Orchestra Plays Mashup of Jewish Popular Melodies

The Sunday Orchestra is an ensemble of professional musicians from different countries, performing hit songs from five continents.

The group consists of string instruments and vocalists. It has participated in the opening ceremonies of various prestigious festivals and exhibitions, as well as corporate events held by the largest Russian and foreign companies, from Vladivostok to Tel Aviv and from Berlin to Bangkok.

In this video clip, the Sunday Orchestra performs a medley of Hebrew and Jewish music, including *Hava Nagila, Bei Mir Bist Du Schein, Siman Tov u'Mazal Tov, David Melech Yisrael*, and *Hevenu Shalom Aleichem.*

Type the URL into your browser address bar to see the video:

https://youtu.be/f-fXI__uY-o

Russian Red Army Chorus Sings Hava Nagila

Hava Nagila continues to spread around the world. In the almost five years that we've been blogging, we have posted 43 versions of this classic Hebrew/Jewish song.

It has shown up in many countries, including some unexpected ones (Scroll down the left column on this page and click on "Hava Nagila" in the Keywords list and you'll see what we mean.)

Russia shows up a few times in the list of Hava Nagila countries, but within Russia there are many different renditions. Here's a version sung by the Russian Red Army Chorus. Known as the Alexandrov Ensemble, it's an official army choir of the Russian armed forces. Founded during the Soviet era, the ensemble consists of a male choir, an orchestra, and a dance ensemble.

Type the URL into your browser address bar to see the video:

https://youtu.be/hnt9jipPWDI

Street Circus Theater Performs Hava Nagila in Venice

As if 25 versions of Hava Nagila weren't enough, we found a new one just posted last week showing a street circus troupe called *Orkestrada Circus* performing this classic song a few days ago in the streets of Venice, Italy.

This is a particuarly jubilant version, as the dancers, dressed in circus costumes, whether for Purim or not, dance wildly through the streets.

Type the URL into your browser address bar to see the video:

https://youtu.be/4ZOSflhqFeg

Jewish Song and Dance Return to Minsk in Belarus

Jewish life is returning to Belarus and its capital, Minsk. After the founding of yeshivot in Volozhin and Mir in the nineteenth century, the Jewish population rose to almost a million in the 1900s.

After the Holocaust, only ten percent remained, many of whom moved to Israel. Recent surveys estimate the population now to be around 50,000.

Belarus was home to many notable Jews, including Shimon Peres, Chaim Weitzman, Menachem Begin, Yitzchak Shamir, Eliezer Ben Yehuda, Rabbi Joseph B. Soloveitchik, Irving Berlin, Marc Chagall, Louis B. Mayer, David Sarnoff, and Ayn Rand.

Jewish organizations are taking root in Belarus, such as community centers, youth organizations, kindergartens, newspapers, magazines, and a web site.

A visible sign of a Jewish awakening is the performance of Jewish music in public places. In our ongoing search for new and unusual interpretations of *Tumbalalaika, Hava Nagila*, and *Hevenu Shalom Aleichem* around the world, we came across the Radzimichy Folk Ensemble of Belarus. In the video below, they sing and dance to the melodies of all three songs, dressed in their traditional folk costumes.

Type the URL into your browser address bar to see the video:

https://youtu.be/zRzO5Rn6kmU

A Unique Hava Nagila: No Music, No Words, Just Tap and Clap

We thought we'd seen every rendition of *Hava Nagila* -- sung in so many languages, danced in so many costumes, until we came across a new contender for the title of most unusual treatment of the universally recognized, much played and much overplayed Jewish song.

This one is a song without lyrics and without music. It's acted out in tap dance and hand clapping by the Chicago Tap Theater. It took us more than one watching to get tuned into the rhythm and follow it closely. But after a few viewings, you can get into it. It helps to sing along to the tapping of the dancers.

Chicago Tap Theatre (CTT) is a young and vibrant dance company with a unique mission to preserve the quintessentially American dance form of tap and to take tap to the next level of creativity and innovation. CTT stands apart from other dance companies by bridging the gap between tap and other forms of concert dance (such as jazz, ballet and modern) by adopting a conceptual, narrative (i.e., story-based) and more emotional approach to its work.

Under the dynamic direction of internationally renowned dancer and choreographer Mark Yonally, CTT has gained a loyal following in its hometown of Chicago and continues to develop and enhance its reputation nationally and around the world.

Type the URL into your browser address bar to see the video:

https://youtu.be/03r5hCGmpTk

A Bold, Energetic Performance of Hava Nagila

Since starting Jewish Humor Central three years ago, we have brought you 25 different versions of Hava Nagila performed all over the world. Sometimes it seems that this is the most overperformed song in the world. Yet we continue to marvel at the new and different interpretations given by singers and dancers in predictable and unpredictable places.

Just a few days ago, a new sensual, energetic version appeared on the Internet, sung and danced by Georgian pop stars Anri Jokhadze and Veriko Turashvili. It moves very fast, and it's hard to read the signs in the background, but it appears to have been recorded in the streets of Jerusalem, inclucding the Old City, and also on the beach in Tel Aviv.

We think it would make a great advertisement for Israeli tourism, and we hope that the Tourism Ministry sees it and uses it to pull in more visitors.

Type the URL into your browser address bar to see the video:

https://youtu.be/CkW_OZLPYMA

Hava Nagila - But With a Completely New Melody

We have heard and posted many versions of Hava Nagila from all around the world, but what they all had in common was the melody, which didn't vary whether it was sung in a burlesque hall in Thailand, a Bollywood movie in Bombay, or by a busking team in the streets of Italy.

Today we found a new version of Hava Nagila, sung to an entirely new melody. The singer is Noah Solomon Chase, a lead singer and guitarist from the band *Soulfarm* that he founded with C. Lanzbom in 1991.

We've liked their music, a mix of Jewish/Middle Eastern, rock, bluegrass, and Celtic influence. We plan to profile *Soulfarm* in a separate blog post soon.

This new melody for Hava Nagila was composed by Cecelia Margules and Rami Yadid.

Type the URL into your browser address bar to see the video:

https://youtu.be/bQ2hV2eyRAY

Hava Nagila Is the Musical Choice Of Engineer In Peru

If you were Paola Patricia Pereda Navarro, one of the 33 engineers who participated in Talent Night at the College of Engineers in Lima, Peru last week, and had to choose music for a dance performance, what song would you pick as your background music? Hava Nagila, of course.

his song keeps turning up in the most unexpected locales, of which the latest is Peru. There's just something about the song that makes it irresistible, whether you're in India, Thailand, Israel, Russia, Texas, the UK, Cuba, or Estonia.

Type the URL into your browser address bar to see the video:

https://youtu.be/A6tO_Redq9E

Hava Nagila Emerges as Popular Theme for Gymnasts

Since we started this blog almost two years ago, we've had a special fascination with the many ways that different cultures have adopted *Hava Nagila* as their very own.

While we haven't found anything more bizarre than the burlesque dancer in Thailand, one of the more popular posts on Jewish Humor Central, we have shared videos of the song performed in India, Italy, the Shetland Islands, Peru, Russia, the United Kingdom, Estonia, Cuba, and as Texas country music.

On Tuesday, Dvora Meyers of JTA reported that the song, originally a Ukrainian folk dance, has become a preferred background piece for gymnasts performing at championship events.

In he JTA piece, Meyers wrote:

Alexandra Raisman, 17, one of the top elite gymnasts in the United States and a member of the 2010 U.S. World Championships team that took the silver medal last year in Rotterdam, will perform her floor exercise routine this weekend to a string-heavy version of the classic Chasidic niggun, or wordless melody. And if she succeeds in making it to London for the Olympic Games in 2012, she plans to perform the routine on the sport's biggest stage.

Raisman, of Needham, Mass., is trained by the Romanian couple, Mihai and Sylvia Brestyan, who coached the Israeli national team in the early 1990s and also is training world vault champion Alicia Sacramone. The coaches and Raisman's mother selected "Hava Nagila" after several exhaustive late-night online searches.

Reisman, a recipient of the Pearl D. Mazor Outstanding Female Jewish High School Scholar-Athlete of the Year Award given out by the Jewish Sports Hall of Fame in New York, says she is proud to be using the Jewish song "because there aren't too many Jewish elites out there."

Even more important to Raisman than the tune's Jewish connotations, however, is the quality it shares with similar folk tunes -- it inspires audience participation.
"I like how the crowd can clap to it," she says.

It's time to clap along to Reisman's routine in the video below. If you really like gymnastics and want to see more, we're also posting videos that Meyers found of four other gymnasts performing to the same tune. Hava Nagila v'nismecha!

Type the URLs into your browser address bar to see the videos:

https://youtu.be/ID2Rl4umsig

https://youtu.be/-IVUIoLBMEg

https://youtu.be/gdrvKLbDzk4

https://youtu.be/OtVN701-To4

A Mexican Mariachi Version of Hava Nagila in Apatzingan

Apatzingán, located in the hot Tierra Caliente valley, in the west-central part of the Mexican state of Michoacán, has received media attention because of the strong presence of notorious, powerful and wealthy drug trafficking cartels.

But it's also the home of some beautiful music, as played by the Apatzingan Real Mariachi Band.

In this video, they perform a Mexican version of Hava Nagila that we're adding to our collection of more than 50 versions.

Type the URL into your browser address bar to see the video:

https://youtu.be/PWnOpuSyvVw

Wall Street Journal: Hava Nagila Has Fallen on Hard Times

Hava Nagila, that old musical standby, the song that used to be played at every Jewish gathering, is increasingly becoming *musica non grata* at weddings, bar and bat mitzvahs, and other festive occasions.

As simchas, or joyous affairs, include longer dance sets playing a variety of Hebrew music, Hava Nagila is rarely played, unless it's a special request from the hosts or guests. The song is becoming an unwelcome cliche among those who listen to a lot of Hebrew music.

Its popularity hasn't diminished in circles where it's played as the token Jewish dance at events where most of the music is American pop and rock. And it remains an iconic symbol of Jewish life as seen in an upcoming exhibit at the Museum of Jewish Heritage and in a documentary that premiered last week at the San Francisco Jewish Film Festival.

Since starting Jewish Humor Central almost three years ago, we have shared 21 videos of traditional and off-beat versions of Hava Nagila showing up in such places as India, Estonia, Korea, Italy, Russia, Paraguay, Peru, Thailand, and the Shetland Islands. And we're not done. You can expect to see more examples of this enduring song performed in still more unexpected places.

Yesterday's Wall Street Journal carried a front page report about the backlash. As Lucette Lagnado reported,

"Hava Nagila," Hebrew for "Let Us Rejoice," has been a staple of Jewish—and some non-Jewish—celebrations for decades. The song often accompanies the hora, a traditional dance-in-the-round that is performed at weddings, bar mitzvahs, engagement parties and other joyful occasions.

As American Jews assimilated, "Hava Nagila," with its dizzying tune that incorporates major and minor modes, became one of the last cultural touchstones of the past. Even the most secular Jews craved it.

It became "the equivalent of a knish," says Henry Sapoznik, an ethnomusicologist at the University of Wisconsin. Incidentally, he considers it to be "a really crummy little tune."

Crummy or not, the melody rang off the walls of catering halls, echoed in big suburban synagogues that sprouted up after World War II and broke into the musical mainstream in the 1950s. Crooner Harry Belafonte made it one of his signature songs. Chubby Checker danced the twist to it. Lena Horne used the melody to deliver a powerful message against racism in a song called "Now." In 1961, Bob Dylan sang his own version—"Talkin' Hava Nageilah Blues"—in a Greenwich Village club.

Some of those earlier interpretations may have boosted "Hava Nagila" into an improbably cool range. Now, a backlash is in full swing.

"It is the cliché of Jewish music," insists Neshoma Orchestra leader Elly Zomick, which does some 200 wedding and bar mitzvah gigs a year. He avoids playing it—along with "The Macarena," "YMCA," and "Sunrise, Sunset"—unless specifically asked.

Among other tunes from the annoyingly redundant banquet-hall repertoire: "The Electric Slide" and the "Chicken Dance."

Rabbi Haskel Lookstein of Kehilath Jeshurun, a large Orthodox congregation on Manhattan's Upper East Side, isn't one to be moved. The body of Jewish musical works, he says, "has gone leagues beyond" the familiar ditties. Yet "no one sings it unless someone in the wedding party has a nostalgia for the old days."

The Journal has posted a video about the worldwide popularity of the song that surprisingly omits any reference to the backlash reported in the front page article. But it's a nice piece of nostalgia that's worth seeing.

Type the URL into your browser address bar to see the video:

http://on.wsj.com/1zBHCO3

Part 4: HEVENU SHALOM ALEICHEM AROUND THE WORLD

Hevenu Shalom Aleichem by A Korean Ensemble

It's not quite as popular as Hava Nagila, but the Hebrew song, *Hevenu Shalom Aleichem,* is also showing up in unexpected locations around the world.

Hevenu Shalom Aleichem may be catching on because of its message of bringing peace, or maybe it's just appealing as a catchy tune, but nevertheless we were surprised to see how performers in so many countries are taking to it.

In this video, a Korean ensemble really gets into the spirit with singing and dancing, and, if you watch past the 3 minute mark, you will see and hear the most popular YouTube Hebrew song sung once again in yet another country.

Type the URL into your browser address bar to see the video:

http://youtu.be/D61loMbQms8

Another Hevenu Shalom Aleichem in Busan, South Korea

Among the over 600 blog posts that we've shared during the past two years have been some expressions of Jewish life and culture in places where you wouldn't expect it. From now on when we encounter one of these, we'll post it under a new category: Jewish Traces in Unexpected Places.

This post is one of these -- a choir in the city of Busan, South Korea made what we would consider an unusual choice for a musical piece to perform -- Hevenu Shalom Aleichem.

Checking with Wikipedia, we found that Jewish Life in Korea was almost nonexistent until American Jewish soldiers arrived with the start of the Korean War.

As Wikipedia puts it,
The first sizable Jewish presence in Korea was during the Korean War, when hundreds of Jewish soldiers participated in the American-led effort to repel a communist attempt to control the whole peninsula. Among the participants was Chaim Potok, who served as a chaplain. His experiences in Korea led to the book, *The Book of Lights and I am the Clay*.

Most of the Jewish community in South Korea resides in Seoul. The community is mostly U.S. military personnel and their families, business people, English-language journalists and teachers, and tourists. The Jewish population is constantly in flux, due to the rotation of U.S. military personnel in the country. While the soldiers have a Jewish chaplain at the Yongsan Army Base, their services are restricted and off-limits to most civilians. At this time, there are no Jewish schools, but a Chabad Rabbi has arrived in Seoul in Passover 2008.

Israel has full diplomatic relations with South Korea, and the sizable Christian population in the country also keeps ties strong between the countries. In August 2005, the Jerusalem Summit promoting Christian support for Israel was held in Seoul. In contrast, neighboring North Korea has no known Jews within its borders, and is openly hostile towards Israel, and currently forbids Israeli tourists and visitors, however Jews of other nationalities (except American) are not banned to enter.

In April 2008, the first Chabad House was established in Seoul under direction of Rabbi Osher Litzman, accompanied by his wife, Mussia Litzman. As there were no synagogues in the country, Jews in Korea would have to go to the U.S. Army base for Shabbat meals and holiday services. Chabad.org news service reported that the Israeli ambassador to South Korea asked three visiting Lubavitch yeshiva students to help arrange for permanent Chabad emissaries. This marks a monumental and welcomed change in South Korea's Jewish history.

We couldn't find any Jewish reference to Busan, where the concert was held. But the choir did a good job with the traditional Hebrew song of welcome.

Type the URL into your browser address bar to see the video:

http://youtu.be/GhV5DbT7lHY

Mayan Children Sing Hevenu Shalom Aleichem in Guatemala

La paz este con nosotros. That's how you say *Hevenu shalom aleichem* in Spanish. How do we know? We came across a YouTube video uploaded by Jeremy Stadlin that shows him teaching a group of youngsters in a Guatemalan village to sing the popular Israeli song, first in Spanish, and then in Hebrew. All this happens while they are dancing in an expanding and contracting circle.

This is the second of a series of renditions of Hevenu Shalom Aleichem from around the world, sometimes in unexpected locales.

Type the URL into your browser address bar to see the video:

http://youtu.be/K0zj1j_XHuw

The Wiggles Sing Hevenu Shalom Aleichem in Australia

The Wiggles, a popular children's entertainment group that started out in Australia 20 years ago, and has been performing worldwide since then, recorded *Hevenu Shalom Aleichem* and included this video as part of their large collection of CDs and DVDs.

Type the URL into your browser address bar to see the video: http://youtu.be/PslN6RX34lA

Japanese Lovers of Israel, Sing Hevenu Shalom Aleichem

Members of the Japanese-based Makuya movement from both Japan and the United States visited the Carmel Forest in Israel in February, where they planted a symbolic carob tree and paid their respects to the people who were killed in the Carmel fire. The Makuya, Christians who are staunch supporters of Israel and the Jewish people, gave a substantial contribution to KKL-JNF for the Carmel rehabilitation campaign.

The Makuya visit Israel every year and march through city streets singing popular Hebrew songs.

As the Jerusalem Post reported during this year's visit:
The Makuya are fervently identified with the cause of Israel, viewing the establishment of the State of Israel and the unification of Jerusalem as a fulfillment of biblical prophecies. “Makuya” is the Japanese equivalent for the Hebrew word mishkan, which refers to the children of Israel's portable shrine in the desert. This name was chosen to express the basic religious orientation of the Makuyas, who emphasize the significance of the personal encounter with the Divine Presence in everyday life.

Here's a look at the Makuya arriving at Ben Gurion airport on one of their trips a few years ago. Landing in the middle of the night didn't stop them from singing a rousing version of *Hevenu Shalom Aleichem* in the airport.

Type the URL into your browser address bar to see the video.

https://youtu.be/RtUR-ec6Z5Q

Part 5: HINEI MA TOV AROUND THE WORLD

Musical Flashback: Harry Belafonte Sings Hinei Ma Tov

Hinei Ma Tov is one of those songs, like *Hava Nagila* and *Hevenu Shalom Aleichem*, that has broken out of the world of Jewish music to achieve popularity in the general culture.

Its lyrics are the first verse of Psalm 133, which reads, "Behold, how good and how pleasant it is for brethren to dwell together in unity!"
יַחַד גַּם אַחִים שֶׁבֶת נָעִים וּמַה טוֹב מַה הִנֵּה

In the 1977 television film *Raid on Entebbe*, Yonathan Netanyahu and Sammy Berg lead the Israeli commandos in singing the refrain while the commandos' plane is en route to rescue the hostages. It is also played during the closing credits.

In 1960 Harry Belafonte performed *Hinei Ma Tov* on a TV program in England that was captured and uploaded to YouTube. We hope you'll enjoy this version.

Type the URL into your browser address bar to see the video.

https://youtu.be/RCzUWap9rmo

Indonesian Choir Sings "Hinei Ma Tov"

Indonesia is a country of 240 million people, 88% of whom are Muslim. Christian religions make up 9 percent of the population, and Hindu, Buddhist, and Animist about 1 per cent each. At last report there were 20 Jews in the country.

So you can imagine our surprise to find a collection of Hebrew songs performed by a chorus at Indonesia's Padjadjaran University.

Earlier this year we posted a video of the same choir singing *Hava Nagila*, a song that seems to have been adopted by just about every country on Earth, whether or not they know what the words mean.

We hope that members of the choir know the meaning of the words of *Hinei Ma Tov*, which are "How good and how pleasant it is for brothers to sit together."

Type the URL into your browser address bar to see the video.

https://youtu.be/YrA9G27xepE

Flash Mobs Erupt Worldwide to "Hinei Ma Tov"

Who would have thought that a 1999 recording of a traditional Hebrew song by a bunch of Jewish choir boys would start a flash mob dance craze around the world?

But that's just what effect the Miami Boys Choir has had on dancers in the streets of cities in America, Canada, Europe, and even Saigon, South Vietnam.

The Miami Boys Choir, founded and directed by Yerachmiel Begun, has moved to Manhattan since releasing its first few recordings.

They are now more popular than ever, and their rendition of *Hinei Ma Tov* on their album *Stand Up!* has struck a chord internationally.

Here is the dance being performed in the streets of Saigon, followed by the original video of the boys singing and dancing in Jerusalem.

Type the URL into your browser address bar to see the video:

https://youtu.be/VS_ofsUeemQ

Blending Bluegrass Music and Jewish Spirit

In addition to introducing our readers to new comedians, from time to time we've been doing the same for new musical groups and highlighting some of their songs.

Today we discovered the new bluegrass group called Nefesh Mountain. Founded by husband and wife team Eric Lindberg and Doni Zasloff, Nefesh Mountain is pioneering this blend of Jewish Americana throughout the country, bringing their unique knowledge and passion for both Jewish and Bluegrass traditions to the fore, singing English and Hebrew songs alike.

As a duo, Doni and Eric alternate lead and harmony vocals while switching between instruments, using the drive of the banjo, intrigue of the guitar, nuance of the mandolin, and visceral sound of the dobro.

You may recognize Doni Zasloff as Mama Doni, the role she has played in producing CD and DVD albums of children's songs. In 2012 we featured her video *Mission Immatzoble* as one of our Passover posts.

Nefesh Mountain conducts Shabbat and holiday services around the USA. Their first album will be released later this year.

Here is one of the songs from the album, Hinei Ma Tov. Type the URL into your browser address bar to see the video:

https://youtu.be/mXmb-rAJ1vc

Part 6: ADON OLAM AROUND THE WORLD

If your synagogue is anything like ours, the Shabbat service ends with Adon Olam. This is usually led by a prepubescent boy with questionable pitch, key, and general singing ability. This is good for the kid educationally, and should be encouraged. Musically, however, it's not the best way to lift spirits for the rest of Shabbat and the week ahead.

But it's not that way around the world. Adon Olam has become a staple of many singers, choruses, bands, and other musical troupes, both in synagogue and on the concert stage.

Adon Olam, the Budapest Klezmer Way

In Budapest, there's a Klezmer group called SabbathSong, with a unique history.

As their leader, Thomas Masa, explains on their website,

In 1998 during the Hebrew language course closing ceremony held in a small synagogue of Budapest we interpreted with my pianist friend, Bence Oromszegi some of our favourite Jewish songs, out of gratitude. The event was recorded by an amateur. By sheer luck, the chief rabbi, Mr. Thomas Raj, listened to the tape and encouraged us to continue more seriously. So we gathered regularly and enlarged the band by new instruments (clarinet, violin, trombone, trumpet, contrabass, accordion, flute).

I sing the songs in original Hebrew and Yiddish language together with my wife, whose beautiful skilled voice gives a very personal and special interpretation of them. Today I can work with 9 wonderful friend musicians, who are mainly symphonic orchestra members.

We hope you find their interpretation as delightful as we did.

Type the URL into your browser address bar to see the video:

http://youtu.be/ct3age-FODY

Welcoming Shabbat with Adon Olam in Brazil

The Hebraica Club is the center of Jewish social life in Rio, and offers sports activities, theater, and special events year-round. In May 2010 they held a Jewish Cultural Festival, with song and dance performances.

Here's how they sing *Adon Olam* in Rio, as sung by the Hebraica Chorus - Coral Kol Haneshama.

Type the URL into your browser address bar to see the video:

http://youtu.be/bME5REX4MTk

Adon Olam, Argentine Style

How do they sing Adon Olam in Argentina? Here is Yehuda Glantz playing it on the charango with the Israel Philharmonic Orchestra and adding a Spanish twist to the familiar song.

The charango is an ethnic South American instrument similar to the ukulele.

Born in Buenos Aires, Argentina, Glantz is a unique and original artist in the Israeli and universal Jewish world art scene. He has created his own musical style, a fusion of hot Latin rhythms, energetic Chassidic rock beats, and Jewish soul music. He plays 14 different traditional and ethnic South American instruments. He also writes, composes, and produces all his music in his studio in Jerusalem, where he has been living with his family since 1979.

Type the URL into your browser address bar to see the video:

http://youtu.be/78nGYFopaAI

Welcoming Shabbat with Adon Olam – A Russian Version,

International opera star Yevgeni Shapovalov – called "the Israeli Pavarotti" by the media in Israel – formed the THREE TENORS FROM ISRAEL in 2005 with his acclaimed operatic colleagues Felix Livshitz and Vladislav Goray.

All originally from the former Soviet Union, Shapovalov and Livshitz now make their homes in Israel, while Goray remains a Ukrainian citizen. Since their 2005 debut, they have given over 100 sold-out concerts in Israel and Europe, delighting audiences with their breathtaking performances, tinged with humor and nostalgia.

Type the URL into your browser address bar to see the video:

http://youtu.be/W-NEbNW9h_s

Adon Olam Forever: John Philip Sousa Wouldn't Believe This!

No Fourth of July celebration would be complete without the playing of John Philip Sousa's march, *Stars and Stripes Forever*. And no All-American Shabbat at Congregation Beth Torah in Granada Hills, California would be complete without the singing of *Adon Olam* to the melody of *Stars and Stripes Forever*, to the accompaniment of drums and cymbals.

Type the URL into your browser address bar to see the video:

http://youtu.be/G9YcD1abvoU

AY Ballet Presents a Beautiful Rendition of Adon Olam

The AY Ballet, based in Chesapeake, VA, is a school for professional ballet training founded by Andrei Yemelianov, who uses a method and syllabus based on the traditions of Russian Classical Ballet.

While the AY Ballet is not a Jewish ballet school, it seems to be focusing on Jewish themes, such as Jewish weddings, the Exodus from Egypt, the covenant with Abraham, and Jewish songs. Here is their interpretation of the Shabbat hymn *Adon Olam*, with vocals in Hebrew and English.

Type the URL into your browser address bar to see the video:

http://youtu.be/eYY70iymIlo

A Do-Re-Mi Version of Adon Olam From Netanya, Israel

Members of Reform Congregation Natan-Ya in (where else?) Netanya, Israel, appear to be enjoying the nice weather in the seaside resort city as they join in the singing of this popular Shabbat song to the tune of *Do-Re-Mi* from *The Sound of Music*.

Type the URL into your browser address bar to see the video:

http://youtu.be/6Vd-UUx6VwE

Adon Olam Around the World: A Brazilian "Hey Jude" Version

Adon Olam, the traditional song that ends the morning Shabbat service in most synagogues, has almost as many versions as *Hava Nagila*.

We've shared more than 20 versions of *Hava Nagila* and eight of *Adon Olam*, two of them from Brazil. The videos and their descriptions are all listed and linked together in our book Jewish Humor on Your Desktop: Jewish Traces in Interesting Places.

Today we're returning to Brazil for a third time, with the *Kol Haneshama* Chorale making their second appearance, this time with an unusual take on *Adon Olam*. It's set to the Beatles' song *Hey Jude*.

This group really gets around. They sing in synagogues, clubs, auditoriums, and other locations in Brazil, not all of them Jewish. If you happen to notice some of the wall hangings in this performance, this will become apparent.

Tomorrow if you're called on to lead the singing at the end of the service, you might consider this version. You'll probably be surprised by the number of congregants singing along.

Type the URL into your browser address bar to see the video.

https://youtu.be/UXN9eSHsQ44

Back to Brazil for a Leaping Version of Adon Olam

Brazil has a tradition of dance troupes performing Israeli dances, especially on Israel Independence Day. This one, called *Lehakat Shalom* (Troupe of Peace), features between 20 and 30 young women (we couldn't get an exact count) who leap in unison with an exuberance that we have never seen in renditions of *Adon Olam* in our own synagogue.

This is certainly an uplifting performance, especially the arms of the dancers, which lift ever higher as the song builds in intensity. Not exactly a typical *Adon Olam* as performed by your typical pre-teen at the end of a Shabbat morning service, but one that we hope will inspire you.

Type the URL into your browser address bar to see the video:

http://youtu.be/ZS77yTa91NE

Adon Olam (Pharrell Williams' "Happy") in Paris Synagogue

Since Pharrell Williams' hit song *Happy* was nominated for an Academy Award in 2014, it's been the basis for many parodies. We posted a few, including exuberant dance moves by residents of Jerusalem, Tel Aviv, and Efrat.

We even posted a Sukkah hop version of the song last month. But we were unprepared for its appearance as the melody for a new version of *Adon Olam* in the *La Victoire* Great Synagogue in Paris.

This is a video that we just had to post because it fits perfectly into two series that we've been running over the last few years, *Adon Olam* Around the World and Unexpected Traces in Jewish Places.

So if you feel especially happy as you leave your synagogue tomorrow, why not surprise your friends by launching into a few choruses of this up to date version of a Shabbat classic?

Type the URL into your browser address bar to see the video.

https://youtu.be/Tf_e23koO_o

Part 7: A-BA-NI-BI AROUND THE WORLD

It Started in Israel, and Then it's off to Malaysia, and Then...

A Ba Ni Bi, a seemingly nonsensical song that won first prize for Israel in the 1978 Eurovision Song Contest, has taken off and found expression in many languages and in many venues that are surely surprising original singer Izhar Cohen, composer Nurit Hirsh, and songwriter Ehud Manor.

A Ba Ni Bi is actually not nonsensical, at least when sung in Hebrew. It gets a little weird when it's sung in Chinese, Spanish, Thai, and other languages.

As Ingalls points out, it's cleverly written in *S'fat HaBet* (B Language,) an Israeli variation of Pig Latin. The phrase *Aba Nibi Obo Hebev Obo Tabach* is simply *Ani Ohev Otach* (I Love You) with the suffixes ba, bi, bo, and beh appended to each syllable. If it were sung in English, the words would be *Iby Lubuve Youboo*. But nobody sings it that way.

Here's a little nostalgia -- the original prize winning performance at the 1978 Eurovision Song Contest, followed by a version of the song performed by bridesmaids at a wedding dinner in Sabah, Malaysia.

Type the URLs into your browser address bar to see the videos:

http://youtu.be/Q8IDx4Hmzho

http://youtu.be/Jeyol8suuCE

A Ba Ni Bi Takes Root In The Far East: Showtime In Singapore!

A Ba Ni Bi has made its way to Singapore, where it was performed on stage at River Hongbao 2010, a nine-day festival celebrating the Chinese New Year and welcoming the Year of the Tiger.

What all this has to do with Hebrew pig latin and silly love song is anybody's guess, but if it brings joy around the world, who can complain?

Type the URL into your browser address bar to see the video:

http://youtu.be/JxJNrS6moko

A Ba Ni Bi Moves on to Spain

El Chaval de la Peca, also known as Marc Parrot Rufias (Barcelona, 1967) is a Catalan singer and composer.

He gained national popularity in the late 90's by remixing old popular Spanish songs.

So what song do you think is one of his most popular songs? You guessed it!

Type the URL into your browser address bar to see the video:

http://youtu.be/Nyc1lBmvIOY

Here's another performance on the popular TV show Cantame Como Paso in Madrid:

http://youtu.be/3w0daF4VOBg

What Does a Venezuelan Pop Star Sing? A Ba Ni Bi

Carlos Baute is a Venezuelan pop singer and television host. What is he singing? You know already.

Type the URL into your browser address bar to see the video:

http://youtu.be/zFFaJHArATU

And on to Iceland

Euroband is the name of an Icelandic technopop and dance duo. Guess what song they brought to Iceland and what song brought them fame in their country?

Type the URL into your browser address bar to see the video:

http://youtu.be/ooZF_pFiFFM

Hot Black Stuff Performs A Ba Ni Bi at Dutch Song Festival

Hot Black Stuff is a pop singing trio in the Netherlands. Here is their version of A Ba Ni Bi.

Type the URL into your browser address bar to see the video:

http://youtu.be/dP0qYDbXx3Y

A Ba Ni Bi: The Choice for Line Dancing

No, it's not the Chicken Dance, it's not the Macarena, and it's not the Tush Push. What is it? A Ba Ni Bi, of course. Our silly Israeli song has become an international hit when it comes to line dancing, a form of dance that's usually associated with Country and Western in the United States.

But line dancing is popularly internationally, both as a form of dance and as a form of exercise. And A Ba Ni Bi has found its place as a standard in the world of line dancing. Here are some examples of line dancers around the world moving and shaking to this Israeli prize winning song from the Eurovision contest in 1978.

Type the URLs into your browser address bar to see the videos:

http://youtu.be/Rt7AQayAaEQ

http://youtu.be/PPuL7Vj7IkQ

http://youtu.be/OeKUbpvE-f4

http://youtu.be/85TKTxChOek

Abanibi Is Still a Big Hit.....in Thailand

A Ba Ni Bi, a seemingly nonsensical song that won first prize for Israel in the 1978 Eurovision Song Contest, has taken off and found expression in many languages and in many venues that are surely surprising original singer Izhar Cohen, composer Nurit Hirsh, and songwriter Ehud Manor.

The song was the subject of an article in Tablet magazine, in which Marjorie Ingalls reflects on the song's explosion onto the Jewish camp scene where it was and still is a staple of the *zimriah* and *rikudiah* (song and dance festvals) that are focal points of the camp season.

A Ba Ni Bi is actually not nonsensical, at least when sung in Hebrew. It gets a little weird when it's sung in Chinese, Spanish, Thai, and other languages. We have posted previous versions of the song performed in Spain, Malaysia, and Singapore.

As Ingalls, points out, It's cleverly written in *S'fat HaBet* (B Language,) an Israeli variation of Pig Latin. The phrase *Aba Nibi Obo Hebev Obo Tabach* is simply *Ani Ohev Otach* (I Love You) with the suffixes ba, bi, bo, and beh appended to each syllable. If it were sung in English, the words would be *Iby Lubuve Youboo*. But nobody sings it that way.

Here is a version of the song performed recently in Thailand. The singers can't pronounce the words in the refrain correctly. The verses are either in Thai or in English. Either way, we can't figure them out. If you can, please let us know in your comments.

Just below, we're sharing the original Hebrew version that won the 1978 Eurovision song contest for Israel. Enjoy!

Type the URL into your browser address bar to see the video:

https://youtu.be/q4MkyCcwPUg

Part 8: TUMBALALAIKA AROUND THE WORLD

Tumbalalaika in Amsterdam's Portuguese Shul

The Yiddish folk love song *Tumbalalaika* originated in Eastern Europe in the 19th century, but its exact origin is hard to pinpoint. That hasn't prevented it from being sung and played over and over, not only in places where Yiddish songs are sung, but just about everywhere in the world, in vocal and instrumental versions, in cabarets and in the movies.

Just as we have followed the songs *Hava Nagila, Adon Olam, Hevenu Shalom Aleichem,* and *Abanibi* as they took different forms as interpreted by a wide variety of singers, musicians, and dancers, we're starting a series today that will bring you many interpretations of this universal courting and love song. We'll post other versions from time to time over the next few months.

We're starting the series with a classic version sung by famed cantors Naftali Herstik, Alberto Mizrachi, and Benzion Miller with the Neimah Singers in a concert "Cantors; A Faith in Song" recorded in the Portuguese Synagogue of Amsterdam in 2003.

Type the URL into your browser address bar to see the video:

https://youtu.be/H4IF8OmLOMw

Yiddish Song Surfaces in Italian Movie

When we started a series a few weeks ago about the popularity of the Yiddish song *Tumbalalaika* we weren't sure where the road would lead as we followed the song around the world. Just like the appearance of *Hava Nagila* in unexpected places, this song is showing up in some surprising locales.

Today we're looking at a 2002 Italian film titled *Prendimi l'anima* (The Soul Keeper) by film maker Roberto Faenza about a love affair between the psychoanalyst Carl Jung and a young Russian Jewish girl, Sabina Spielrein. Here's a summary of the plot:

In 1905 a 19-year-old Russian girl suffering from severe hysteria is admitted into a psychiatric hospital in Zurich. A young doctor, Carl Gustav Jung, takes her under his care and for the first time experiments with the psychoanalytical method of his teacher, Sigmund Freud. Based on recently exposed secret correspondence between Jung, Freud and Sabina Spielrein, this true story begins with the Spielrein's healing, closely related to her passionate love affair with Jung, followed by her return to post-revolutionary Russia where she became Switzerland's first female psychoanalyst.

So what does this have to do with *Tumbalalaika?* Beats us. But the song is the musical background of the last five minutes of the film as it plays repeatedly in a sequence where the doctors and patients of the asylum dance to its haunting melody.

Type the URL into your browser address bar to see the video:

https://youtu.be/tjV3tXXydEQ

Igor Epstein Plays Tumbalalaika in Rostov, Russia

As we follow the Yiddish folk song *Tumbalalaika* around the world, featuring performances in Amsterdam and in an Italian movie, we come to Rostov, Russia, probably not far from where the song originated.

Last month, the Jewish community of Rostov was the site of a concert that featured violinist Igor Epstein playing *Tumbalalaika* in the Gorky Theater. With a black kippah nestled in his mane of white hair, Epstein showed his virtuosity in interpreting this folk classic.

Rostov-on-Don has a population of 1.1 million people including over 10,000 Jews. Once home to a bustling Jewish community, Rostov now has just one Synagogue around which Jewish communal activities are centered.

Rostov has been the site of tragic events, including anti-Jewish riots in 1883, the pogrom of 1905, and a Nazi massacre in 1943. Rostov-on-Don is also noted for the resting place of the fifth Lubavitcher Rebbe, Tzadik Rabbi Sholom Ber Schneerson (Rabbi Rashab) of righteous memory, who spent the final years of his life in this city.

Today Jewish life is experiencing a revival in Rostov. Two years ago a major restoration of the shul was completed. Currently they have a daily morning minyan and Shabbat services attended by more than 100 people. There is also a Jewish day school with more than 130 children enrolled.

Type the URL into your browser address bar to see the video:

https://youtu.be/NcVKnQiqOos

Tumbalalaika in a Mexican Cafe

The Yiddish folk love song *Tumbalalaika* originated in Eastern Europe in the 19th century, but its exact origin is hard to pinpoint.

That hasn't prevented it from being sung and played over and over, not only in places where Yiddish songs are sung, but just about everywhere in the world, in vocal and instrumental versions, in cabarets and in the movies.

Just as we have followed the songs *Hava Nagila, Adon Olam, Hevenu Shalom Aleichem,* and *Abanibi* as they took different forms as interpreted by a wide variety of singers, musicians, and dancers, we're continuing this series that we started in 2012 that will bring you many interpretations of this universal courting and love song. We'll post other versions from time to time.

This version was recorded by the instrumental group Trio Nu in the Idish Cafe in Mexico.

Type the URL into your browser address bar to see the video:

https://youtu.be/WAAkgQTJQlQ

Yiddish Cabaret at the Blue Note Club in Milan

OK, we know, it's a long way to go to see five women in glittering gold gowns singing Yiddish songs, playing piano, violin, and cello. But where else but a jazz club in Milan, Italy can you see such an ensemble in action? And the music, the music! Tumbalalaika, Dona Dona, Der Neier Sher, and Yiddish wedding music.

The performers call their act *Di Goldene Pave* (pronounced pav-eh) - In Yiddish, The Golden Peacock. The act recently premiered at the Blue Note cabaret/jazz club in Milan. This group consists of five professional musicians/singers coming from different European countries. The quintet does vocals, light percussion, violin, viola, cello, piano as well as backing vocalists, playing all the different flavors of Jewish music, from Klezmer to Yiddish songs to Spanish/Sephardi music, to Yemenite folk song.

The *Goldene Pave* are:

Angelica Dettori: vocals and light percussions
Luviona Hasani: violin and backing voice
Eriola Gripshi: viola and backing voice
Cecilia Salmé: cello and backing voice
Valentina Verna: piano and backing voice

And you really don't have to travel to Italy to see them. Here is their version of Tumbalalaika.

Type the URL into your browser address bar to see the video:

https://youtu.be/PapAvrnyVZg

Mike Burstyn: Tumbalalaika as a Yiddish Lesson

In November 2012 we started a series tracking the Yiddish song *Tumbalalalaika* around the world, sharing versions performed in Amsterdam, Milan, Russia, and Belarus.

In 2009 Yiddish actor and singer Mike Burstyn performed the song at Kehilath Israel Synagogue in Overland Park, Kansas.

The concert was one of a series of events celebrating the traditional synagogue's 100th anniversary. Burstyn presented the song in the form of a Yiddish lesson, by translating the song from Yiddish to English. Bur judging from the audience reaction, they didn't need much translation.

Type the URL into your browser address bar to see the video:

https://youtu.be/clt1XQoYwaE

A NOTE FROM THE AUTHOR

IF YOU ENJOYED THIS BOOK, YOU CAN GET MY OTHER JEWISH HUMOR BOOKS AT AMAZON.COM

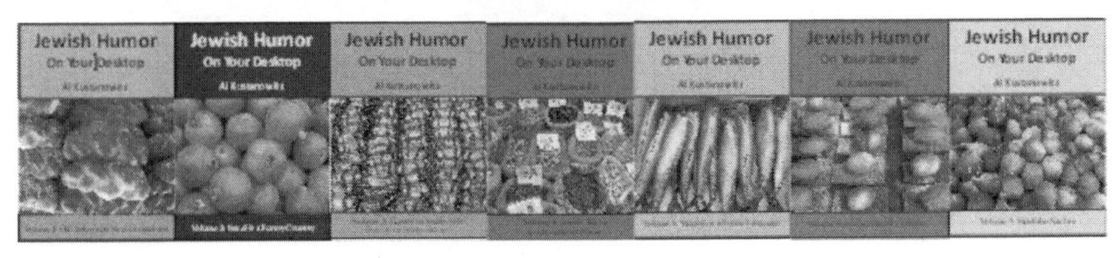

I hope you enjoyed reading the anecdotes in this book and watching the videos that they link to. I am available for presentation of this material to your synagogue, JCC, or other organization in the form of lectures and entertaining programs on Jewish humor that survey the broad range of topics in these books or focus on the individual categories.

If you would like more information about these lectures, please look at my website on Jewish humor programs, www.JewishHumorPrograms.com and contact me via email at akustan@gmail.com.

Al Kustanowitz
Publisher and Blogger-in-Chief
Jewish Humor Central
www.JewishHumorCentral.com

29203744R00109

Made in the USA
Middletown, DE
15 February 2016